CRUISING
UNDER SAIL

CRUISING
UNDER SAIL

Dag Pike

ADLARD COLES NAUTICAL
B L O O M S B U R Y
LONDON · NEW DELHI · NEW YORK · SYDNEY

PUBLISHED IN ASSOCIATION WITH

PANTAENIUS
Yacht Insurance

Published by Adlard Coles Nautical
an imprint of Bloomsbury Publishing Plc
50 Bedford Square, London WC1B 3DP
www.adlardcoles.com

ISBN 978-1-4081-8189-8
ePDF 978-1-4081-8191-1
ePUB 978-1-4081-8190-4

A CIP catalogue record for this book is available from
the British Library.

This book is produced using paper that is made
from wood grown in managed, sustainable forests.
It is natural, renewable and recyclable. The logging
and manufacturing processes conform to the
environmental regulations of the country of origin.

Photos on pages 3, 6–7, 36–37, 96–97, 116–117,
128–129, 140–141, 150–151, 152–153, 160–161,
167 top, 171 and 186–187 from Jeanneau, with thanks.
Also thanks to Bavaria yachts and all others who
helped with photos.

Designed by CE Marketing
Page layouts by Susan McIntyre
Typeset in 10 on 12pt Helvetica light condensed

Printed and bound in China by C&C offset printing Co

Contents

Introduction

The freedom of cruising

Cruising in a sailboat is so much more than just a journey undertaken without the constraints of a strict schedule – for me, it's all about enjoyment, visiting new and exciting places, and getting pleasure and satisfaction from making the passage itself.

Many people these days are attracted to cruising, but so often they do it on a large cruise ship, with perhaps 3,000 other people, and their main ambition seems to be taking a tour of the local sights on the days spent in port. Of course there can be pleasure in that – but not for me. I love the idea of planning and plotting a cruise, with the pleasure shared equally between time spent at sea and time spent in harbour. When sailboat cruising, you are doing things entirely on your own terms, and at the same time utilising mainly natural resources to achieve your goals. Sailboat cruising is probably the greenest form of travel, harnessing natural resources to travel at your own pace and go where you want to go – which some may see as a bonus and others as a challenge.

Whatever your level of experience you can find an option that meets your requirements – maybe a gentle cruise in daylight in fine weather, or a more challenging overnight cruise in busy waters. In your early days of cruising you might want to start in familiar waters in daylight and fine conditions, and then graduate to more challenging cruises, such as going foreign or cruising at night. There are the easy options of cruising from marina to marina or the more challenging cruises using night anchorages and hidden harbours. The joy of sailboat cruising is that there are so many options and the choice is yours. When you are using the wind as your motive power, you are not limited in range like people cruising on powerboats – except, of course, with your water and food supplies.

With this freedom comes a responsibility. On land, responsibility for your actions is vested in countless rules and regulations and your personal decision-making is limited. The International Maritime Organization's Regulations for the Prevention of Collision at Sea (COLREGs, see chapter 13) guide your actions when another vessel gets close, and there are a few no-go areas where certain requirements – usually military – might restrict your actions, but in the main you are free to roam the seas at your own pace and in your own time. Of course, the winds will influence what you can or cannot do – but then negotiating with the weather is part of the challenge.

The safety of your boat, its navigation, and your crew are among your responsibilities at sea. If you are organised about it, these need not be onerous; but you do need to consider how you will deal with the demands and responsibilities of a cruise. This is what this book is all about – demonstrating how to embark on and execute a cruise in a seamanlike manner and how to get maximum fun and satisfaction from doing it.

For me, half the fun and excitement is in the planning. Get this right, and when you actually set off on your cruise, all the elements should fall into place. Careful and detailed planning can help pass the long winter nights and here you can explore not only all the options but also the permutations of weather and tides. One of the major aspects of taking responsibility for a cruise is establishing the level of risk involved and the level of certainty you want for your cruise; there will be more about this later. You could set off with no particular destination in mind or have every detail planned beforehand. Most people

Anchored off a sandy beach in perfect weather.

'...the joy of sailboat cruising is that there are so many options.'

will choose a path somewhere between the two, and of course you can always mix and match. My choice has been to go for a good measure of flexibility so that you can adapt to changes in the weather; but such flexibility is not always possible if you plan to use marinas, where booking a berth beforehand is often necessary.

The weather will dictate much of what you can do and where you can go on your cruise, and weather is the one thing you cannot plan in advance. It can and will change in the short term, so a measure of flexibility in your plans is essential. At times the weather can cooperate and fit in perfectly with what you have planned, but you will only know that at the time. My approach is always to plan a cruise in advance but to build in some time margins so you can be flexible if things don't work out as planned. The weather is such a critical aspect of cruising that I have devoted a whole chapter of this book just to that subject and how you can fine-tune weather forecasts to get a much better idea of what is possible and practical. At times there may be a storm raging overhead and even if the seas are sheltered you will hesitate to go. In many respects, with sailboat cruising you are less interested in the sea conditions and much more interested in the wind strength and direction. The wind will dictate not only when you can go and how you can go but also the level of risk that might be involved – a very important factor in planning and executing a cruise.

I love daydreaming about where I'd like to go cruising and wish I could visit all the places on my list. It doesn't cost much to be an armchair sailor, and maybe that is a hobby to save for my old age! Turning such dreams into reality is part of the challenge of cruising and of course it requires a considerable degree of commitment if that reality is to be an enjoyable cruise. There is an army of cruising people who relish the challenge of a more difficult cruise, perhaps having to overcome adversity in a way that doesn't happen on shore. Many of the potential risks are under your control so you can decide the level of risk you want to experience.

Choosing your cruising style

One of the basic choices when planning a cruise is whether to hop from marina to marina or take the more adventurous option of anchoring or mooring in port or even in remote bays. The marina option has much to recommend it because it means you can step ashore each night for a meal, visit a bar, take a shower and go shopping, as well as top up with fresh water. Using anchorages, or even tying up to a mooring buoy in harbour, means you will need to be a lot more independent. It will mean going ashore in a tender, which many people find an attractive option because it is like cutting off your ties with the shore and becoming fully dependent on your own resources – part of the escape scenario that can be the main attraction of cruising.

'…turning such dreams into reality is part of the challenge of cruising.'

If you are going down the route of more adventurous cruising, your tender will play an important part in what you can and cannot do. Apart from going ashore in harbour, a capable tender opens up the way for more exciting cruising – taking the tender up rivers and into tiny harbours and coves that are not directly accessible with your sailboat because of its draft. I love this type of exploration and it can take you to places that the world has virtually passed by. So the tender should be considered an essential part of a cruising yacht, something that can extend your cruising horizons.

Most people, when they think of cruising, think of a boat that has night accommodation so that when you get to harbour you can sleep on board and have access to a bathroom of sorts and cooking facilities. That is the luxury side of modern cruising; but there is a hardier breed of cruising devotees who still do their cruising in the traditional way on board boats with very limited facilities. You can still do cruising where you fill up with fresh water from a stream on the shore and where your anchor becomes your best friend. Bypass the marinas and find the hidden coves, the remote sheltered bays, and you enter the realm of what I call adventure cruising. This can be both exciting and rewarding, and it takes you back to the basics of sailboat cruising. There is another option where you can combine this sort of adventure in the daytime, coping with a variety of sea conditions and challenging navigation situations during the day, with making harbour and staying in hotels with the luxury of a hot bath and a hot meal at night. The choices are yours.

A night at anchor can produce magnificent sunsets.

The right yacht for the job

Your style of cruising will depend to a certain extent on the type of sailboat you are using. A sailboat that is efficient for getting the maximum speed out of the prevailing winds may not make the ideal cruising yacht – this type of cruiser/racer can provide exciting sailing, but you may find that the draft of a fixed keel can limit your access to some harbours and you will not be able to dry out in tidal harbours. A twin keel or a centreboard yacht may

Cruising in the sun with a good breeze. One of life's pleasures, but with pleasure comes responsibility.

be much better for access to harbours off the beaten track but it will not provide the same exciting sailing. The style of yacht you decide on will have a considerable influence when it comes to both planning and executing a cruise. Also, if more challenging sailing is your passion, you might also need to consider a stronger crew.

'...let go the ropes, and head off into a world of interest and excitement.'

I doubt whether the perfect cruising yacht has yet been designed; however, you can make the best of what you have by fully understanding how your yacht behaves at sea, and this is where experience really counts. When you are at sea, analysing what is happening to the yacht as it encounters different wind and wave conditions will give you a better understanding of both the boat and the sea conditions. Try experimenting with different sail settings and different angles into the wind – you may find that even small changes in the heading can make a considerable difference to how the yacht performs. In this way you will gradually build up a familiarity with the behaviour of your yacht and this experience will not only help you to get the best performance and the most comfortable ride from the boat in any given conditions but could also prove very valuable if you encounter unexpected adverse weather.

For safe cruising, you also need to be familiar with the on-board systems – knowing how the engine, electrics, electronics, plumbing and, perhaps most of all, the sails work, and what the various alarms mean when they sound, gives you a measure of confidence that in the event of any emergency you will find a solution. Spending an afternoon crawling round the boat with the owner's manual can reap rewards when you need to find a solution to a problem.

Once you have a good feel for the workings of your boat and how it performs at sea, all you need to do is plan where you want to go, check the weather and tides, let go the ropes, and head off into a world of interest and excitement.

1

Preparing to cruise

The joy of paper charts

Half the fun of cruising is in the planning – working out where you want to go, looking at the feasibility of different routes and different ports, and perhaps planning to go to places you have not visited before. You can while away many happy hours this way in the winter, and these days there is so much information on the Internet that you can do what amounts to a virtual cruise without even leaving the comfort of your computer desk. Of course, this can take some of the fun out of the process, because the planning becomes almost too easy and nothing is left to the imagination – I still love the idea of spreading out the paper charts on the table, poring over them with a glass of whisky in my hand, and dreaming of places to visit in the sun…

This may be a romantic view of planning a cruise, but for me it has always been the way to work. The joy of working on a paper chart is that you have a much wider view of the area you will be cruising in – you get a much better feeling for the layout of the sea and the land than you can with a computer screen. It's much easier to visualise the cruising area and to see the beginning and the end of a day's cruise. On a computer screen the scale becomes so small that you lose much of the detail, while the screen itself seems to erect a barrier between you and the points of interest, so that much of the emotion and excitement is lost.

Although I love the electronic systems that have transformed modern navigation, paper charts are surely a work of art – they are a masterpiece of graphic display and there is so much information and detail on one sheet of paper. You should carry paper charts anyway as a back-up to the electronic systems, and using them at the planning stage of a cruise will familiarise you with the process, and probably give you a good deal of pleasure too.

When you have completed the planning, you can transfer the information to the electronic system if you prefer. We all have own way of carrying out the planning, but what is important is that you do it.

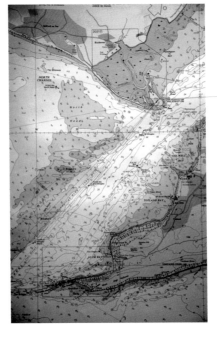

Above: Half the fun of cruising is in the planning of the voyage.

Left: Much of the detailed information can be missing from large scale charts.

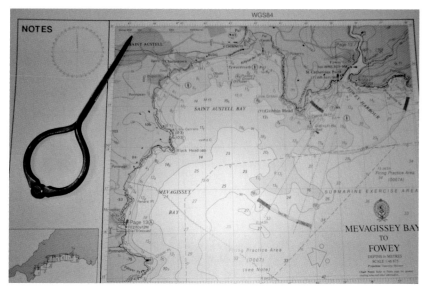

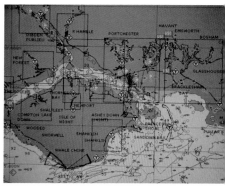

Above: It is important to get the scale right when using electronic charts.

Left: You can see the big picture when using paper charts.

The general plan

There are two levels to planning for a cruise. The first is just to get a general idea of where you want to go and how you want to achieve this, and the second is the detailed passage planning, which we will look at in Chapter 2. This element must be done within a day or so of departing, or even on the day you leave, because the weather will always play a significant part and you need up-to-date information on that. When you are under sail the wind strength and direction will govern your progress to the point where you become almost obsessed by the weather forecasts.

Translating what you see on the chart into the full picture can be easier with the photo images that come with electronic charts.

So what is involved in the general plan? Say you have a week for the cruise and you have to be back at your home port by a certain day. For this you will need to build in some reserve of time so that in the event of adverse winds and conditions you will not find yourself under pressure to get back and perhaps take unnecessary risks to meet a deadline. One of the major reasons people get into trouble at sea is that they take risks to complete a passage because of time restraints, even when the weather and sea conditions suggest that staying put might be the wise thing to do. With modern weather forecasts you get a pretty good idea of what the weather will be like about three days ahead, so halfway through your cruise you can assess whether you can continue in comfort or need to consider cutting things short and heading home.

There are so many small anchorages and harbours to visit.

If you plan a simple out-and-back route, you will find yourself at the furthest distance from your home port on the day that reliable weather forecasts become available for the final day of the cruise. At this point you will have run out of many of your options because there is only one way to get home and you need the full three days to do that. A cruise of this type has its attractions but does not allow you any flexibility or room to negotiate with the weather if things turn sour. You tend to feel increasingly under pressure the further you are from home, so this is probably not a relaxing approach to cruising. Much better to build in flexibility at the early planning stage – think about a triangular cruise, for example, which will allow you to cut off one of the corners if you need to save a day or make up time from any delays.

Most out-and-back cruises follow a coastline route and it is easy to see the attraction of this. You are not faced with any long passages where you have nowhere to run to if things go wrong and with coastal cruising there is usually a convenient harbour close at hand if you change your mind or are uncomfortable with the conditions. With triangular cruising, you can still include some coastal cruising if you plan things carefully. For example, you could leave from the south coast of England and head across the English Channel. Once there you can do your coastal cruising with the option of heading home across the Channel early if the forecast turns sour. You can do the same in the Irish Sea, and in the Mediterranean there are many fascinating islands you could include on your itinerary, which would then allow you to vary your plans according to the weather.

The tender can be a vital piece of your equipment when cruising.

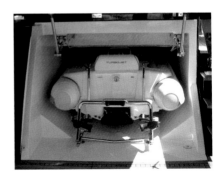

Another alternative is to plan to spend one day exploring a river or an estuary somewhere near the halfway point of the cruise, so that you can leave out this section if you need to gain time. Allowing such margins in your cruise timetable will result in a far more relaxed cruise.

Organising a marina berth

One of the dilemmas you face when planning a cruise is that at busy times it is often necessary to book a marina berth some time ahead. This is where you need to decide what sort of cruising you plan to do. There is much to be said in terms of convenience for making day trips from marina to marina, provided you book ahead. You arrive in harbour knowing you have a berth waiting, and you can just tie up and stroll ashore for a drink or a meal. All services such as shore power, water and even a telephone or Wi-Fi connection are available, and it can be almost like living ashore, except for the sea voyages between ports. Cruising at this level of luxury and convenience will be attractive to some, but the downside is that your carefully planned bookings will be out of sequence if you have to vary your itinerary because of adverse weather. If you like the security of booking ahead, you can always do this and cancel on the day if necessary.

Alternatively, you can arrive in a harbour on spec and hope to find somewhere to moor up. This can take some of the relaxation out of the cruise because you will be on tenterhooks when you reach your destination about where you can moor up. However, it does open up a more flexible approach to cruising and you can change your plans as and when you feel like it or as the weather might dictate. You could perhaps compromise by phoning your next port of call before you leave in the morning to arrange a berth. It is certainly good to be able to tie up alongside at night and stroll ashore, but the uncertainty of finding a berth can make life difficult.

Motor sailing can help you meet deadlines for arrival.

It can be hard to find a mooring at busy times in popular harbours.

Anchoring in a cove

Even out of the way coves can be full of moorings these days.

Another option is to find a quiet anchorage for the night. In the past you could find an anchorage in a harbour, but these days most harbours are crowded with moorings, leaving little or no space to anchor – in fact, anchoring has become almost a forgotten art. What I mean by anchoring is that you find a quiet cove along the coast, move in and drop your anchor, and spend a quiet night in peaceful surroundings.

The tender can be used for exploring in harbours.

This is real cruising, where the boat becomes effectively your self-sufficient home. In this situation, you must be prepared to be totally self-contained – having adequate water on board, doing your own cooking, and perhaps, on modern boats, running a generator to provide power for the cooking or battery charging. You still need to plan for this because you have to ensure that you have adequate food and water on board – you can't easily nip ashore for more.

You need to choose your anchorages with care. A quiet anchorage will depend a great deal on what the wind is doing and is forecast to do; most anchorages are only protected from winds from a certain direction. When you are planning your cruise months in advance, you will have no idea about the likely wind direction beyond knowing the prevailing wind for the region. This means that if you are intending to anchor rather than mooring in a harbour, you will need to have some alternatives available in case your chosen anchorage proves unsuitable.

> *'...see nature in a way you will never see it in harbour.'*

This approach comes under the banner of 'adventure cruising', but to me anchoring is an exciting option where you are free from the noise and bustle of the shore and can watch the sunsets (and perhaps the sunrises) and see nature in a way you will never see it in harbour. This is real cruising as it was 50 years ago and it still has a lot to commend it in terms of satisfaction and sense of achievement – it is all a question of your level of experience and how much excitement or uncertainty you want, and only you can decide that. For the novice, the safe option is the marina cruise, running only during daylight hours; but as you gain experience there are other options to make a cruise more adventurous and fulfilling. The strength of your crew will have a bearing on your plans, and if you are just a couple you will need to be sure you don't extend your capabilities beyond the point of reason. A strong crew of perhaps four or more experienced people can tackle the more arduous conditions and come up smiling at the end.

A small cruising yacht can offer a lot of flexibility in your cruising plans.

Cruising considerations

Cruise planning would be so much easier if you could also plan what the wind would be doing months ahead, but even in the short term the wind is rarely reliable. However, you can consider a wide variety of cruising scenarios.

When deciding on the nature and location of your cruise, much depends on the type of boat you own. If your boat is a cruiser/racer, you may well want to plan your cruise to participate in regattas and races along the way. If the boat can dry out at a mooring, you can think about some of the small and intriguing harbours to be found on coastlines. The speed of the boat may also be a consideration, with a cruiser/racer perhaps capable of averaging 6 or 7 knots per hour and a small yacht perhaps half of that. Each type of cruising yacht has its own personality and its good and bad points, so when planning your cruise it helps to be familiar with these and try to work within any limitations imposed by the design.

When your speed per hour is only in single figures, obviously your daily mileage will be quite low, and even with a cruiser/racer it will only be in the region of 60 miles on a good day with a favourable wind. In light winds and with a smaller yacht, 20 miles a day might be as much as you can comfortably achieve. Try not to be over-ambitious and put yourself under too much pressure, because you will not only take some of the pleasure out of the cruise but may also find yourself taking unnecessary risks. If you plan your cruise anticipating light winds and slow progress, you will have a good margin to play with if the winds are stronger and favourable, and if you make better progress you will have the bonus of more time in harbour.

The cruising boats

There are three main choices for cruising sailboats – the blue water yacht, designed to cope with most conditions found at sea; the comfortable cruising yacht, where the accent is on living on board in considerable style; and the cruiser racer, where the interior may be a bit more spartan but the performance is at the top end. Each has its own personality, so when you are planning your cruise it helps to understand their good and bad points.

The blue water cruising yacht

The fixtures and fittings in a blue water cruising yacht are on the rugged side because failure under extreme weather conditions is not acceptable. This is the type of sailboat that appeals to people who are thinking in terms of extended cruises, perhaps being at sea for several days at a time rather than running from port to port. It could be argued that a blue water yacht is for the serious cruising man, who has time to spend on cruises lasting for weeks rather than days, and for whom the enjoyment comes as much from the days at sea as the days in harbour. The hull shape of such yachts tends to be more along the classic lines of a long keel yacht in order to give a more sea-kindly motion. Obviously performance is important in every sailboat these days, but with a blue water cruiser performance will not be the total focus of the design.

The comfortable cruising yacht

The comfortable cruising yacht is the choice of most cruising sailors and there has been enormous development in this style of yacht in recent years. The hull forms have expanded in shape in order to create more internal space and the interiors have changed out of all recognition over the last 40 years. Even in a 35 footer you can find a serious galley with the capacity to produce full three-course meals and a bathroom with space to move around. Headroom is important for comfort inside and is given priority even in quite small yachts, resulting in a high coachroof; and the level of finish really impresses. It has to be said that the focus of many modern designs in this category is

A catamaran offers higher sailing speeds and a reduced craft.

towards the interior, but clever design and evolvement has allowed this to be combined with adequate sailing performance. The hull forms have changed from being narrow and deep to a wider, more spacious shape and straight stems are now almost a standard feature, inherited from racing boats, in order to increase the waterline length, which in turn helps to increase the hull speed. A notable

The underwater hull of a typical cruising yacht with a fixed draft.

The classic motor sail style of yacht makes you less dependant on the wind.

feature is the way in which the traditional lovely sheer line that dipped amidships has been replaced by a reverse sheer. This is not so pretty but it does give more space or headroom inside the boat without spoiling the sailing qualities.

The motor sailer

Today, the motor sailer style of sailboat has almost disappeared as far as the name is concerned, but it still exists in the form of sailboats with a full wheelhouse or a fixed cuddy combined with a powerful engine. From a comfort point of view there is much to be said for the weather protection that is offered, and if you plan to sail during the winter months then this could well be the yacht of choice. The wheelhouse or cuddy does tend to isolate you to a certain extent

Hull shape

In terms of hull shape there are so many options, most of them focused on the shape of the keel – from the long deep keel of tradition to the thin bulb keel of the racing boat and every shape in between. The shape of the keel can influence the type of cruising you undertake, partly because draft can be an important consideration and partly because it will determine the performance. With a fin keel, there will be little or no chance of drying out at a mooring, and a marina or an anchorage will be the logical choice for an overnight stay. Few conventional sailboat hulls can dry out comfortably these days, and if you plan to explore hidden and small harbours on your cruise then something like a bilge keeler or a centreboard yacht might be the best option. This choice is likely to be determined by where you normally keep the boat moored because so many permanent moorings are based in rivers and estuaries that dry out over the tide. There are no such problems in the tideless Mediterranean but then anchoring and mooring are less of an option here.

A modern classic style with the focus on a large open cockpit.

from the outside world, and it can be more difficult to access the necessary ropes for sailing, but sailboat design is always about compromise and the motor sailer is one solution that will appeal to many.

Modern design allows this full height wheelhouse to be combined with good sailing qualities.

The bilge keel yacht was developed primarily for those who have to or want to dry out over a tide and their cruising areas tend to be the tidal regions of the world. In the Mediterranean there is virtually no tide and marinas and anchorages abound, so there would be little call for a bilge keeler in these areas. With bilge keels there will be a loss of performance compared with a deep keel yacht but for many this is an acceptable compromise. The centreboard or lifting keel yacht is another compromise solution and with the keel down there should

A drop keel can be a good compromise on cruising yachts.

be acceptable sailing performance; but you have to consider the additional complication of the lifting mechanism and the space for the board/keel when lifted. An alternative is for the yacht to have a relatively shallow fixed keel and for the centreboard or drop keel to extend down from this and stow within the fixed keel when raised.

We must not forget the multihull cruising yachts, which have a strong and dedicated following. There is so much logic in the concept of a multihull that it is surprising there are not more around; but like most things to do with yacht design, you have to accept compromises with a multihull cruising yacht, be it a catamaran or a trimaran. Yes, you can get a faster boat speed, you are not carrying a load of ballast around to keep the yacht upright, and they can dry out comfortably; but the accommodation may not be the most comfortable in the smaller sizes of multihull as it has to be squeezed into the narrow hulls, and perhaps the biggest snag is that you have to pay a lot more for a marina berth because of the space the yacht occupies. Multihull yachts tend to attract dedicated owners who swear by the concept and are prepared to put up with the downsides in order to get fast cruising at perhaps twice the speed of a conventional

Catamarans offer good upright cruising and performance but the below deck accommodation can be constricted.

sailboat. The ability to sail at 10 or even 12 knots in a good breeze means you can cover significant distances, and with many harbours offering moorings where you can swing around a buoy at no extra charge there is certainly considerable attraction for this concept. Many blue water sailors use multihulls for their cruising yacht and have made extensive ocean passages where the extra speed is a bonus.

What is your aim?

One of the things you have to decide when planning a cruise is how you want to approach it. Is it the time at sea that is important, shaking off the shackles of the shore, enjoying the freedom of the open sea and exercising your sailing skills? Some people get enjoyment from sailing the yacht to the best of their ability, and one of the joys of sailing is the intimacy you can have with your yacht. It can become almost an extension of your personality, the vehicle you use to harness the power of the wind. There is a strong user input into sailboat operation that is rarely found in powered craft and many find great cruising satisfaction from this source.

Or are you undertaking the cruise so you can visit a number of new ports and harbours? For the latter, you might want to allow for more time in harbour and even build in rest days so that you can explore the local environment. You can plan a day in harbour and use the tender to explore a river or creek or just go for a picnic.

Shaking off the shackles of the shore.

The thing with cruising is that it should be done for pleasure and only you can decide where you will obtain maximum enjoyment. There are those who may want to linger in harbour and those who want a leisurely time at sea – and it most cases it can be a bit of both. Then there are those whose challenge comes from the maximum distance covered in a week, from completing a passage under tough conditions and being able to hold their head high in the yacht club afterwards. At the other end of the scale, if you are a bit uncertain of your ability to cope out there on your own, there are cruises in company that can offer a solution where support is close at hand.

The practicalities of cruising

There are also, of course, the more pragmatic things to consider, such as obtaining fuel, water and food, and how much of each will be needed. My experience of stocking up in many ports and harbours around the world is that it can take far longer than you anticipate. With a sailboat and some careful planning, you can be pretty self-sufficient for several days if you want it that way. Of course, you may encounter a patch of calms or light winds and have to use the engine more than you planned in order to keep to some sort of schedule, and it is important to remember that having adequate fuel on board is a great safety feature if circumstances at sea change, so you should try to have a good reserve at all times. If you need to refuel, build in plenty of time – and never ever let the levels drop so low that you can't make harbour for fuel if the planned stops do not work out or the weather takes a turn for the worse.

Fresh water is not such a problem as it is usually laid on in marina berths, but if you plan to anchor on some of your overnight stops you will need to build in time for picking up water and perhaps fresh food at some point.

An overnight passage

' …Cruising at night is not something to undertake lightly.'

So far we have talked about planning your cruise in a series of daylight hops and spending nights in harbour or at anchor. That is the format most people enjoy and plan for; but bear in mind the possibilities of making an overnight passage so that you arrive the next morning at a new destination. There are so many pleasures to be found in an overnight passage – watching the sun set and then rise again, and seeing the huge vista of stars that can appear when you move away from the lights of the land.

Cruising at night is not something to undertake lightly and is best done after some experience with daytime cruising, but it can be very rewarding. It does require more planning and a later chapter in this book covers night cruising in detail. You can, of course, make an overnight passage along the coast but then you miss out on many of the sights and scenery you would have seen in daylight. The best overnight passages are those that take you into open water, perhaps across the English Channel or the Irish Sea or in the Mediterranean, making the passage out to one of the many islands such as Corsica or Sardinia. I have watched the moon rising on one horizon and the sun setting on the opposite horizon in the Mediterranean, the sort of sight you will never see on land. There can also be a huge pleasure in making a landfall at dawn, even with modern electronic navigation that keeps you constantly informed about your position. Bear in mind when planning an overnight cruise that you need an experienced crew so that people can get some sleep on the way.

Fine-tuning the plan

Cruise planning is the early stage of organising what you want to do and where you want to go. It can be valuable to revisit your plan a few days before departure and to feed in the latest information about the forecast weather and what the tides will be doing. This will enable you to fine-tune the programme and to have a better handle on what is possible. These days the Internet is a wonderful source of information about the weather and it is possible to get forecasts stretching ten days ahead. You need to take these with a slight pinch of salt because no forecast for ten days ahead is going to be completely accurate, but they can give a guide, including an idea of the probable wind direction. This can be a great help, because if necessary you can reverse the direction of your cruise so that with luck and a bit of planning the wind will be from a more favourable direction, allowing you to take maximum advantage of the conditions and not make life on board too uncomfortable.

Weather-watching

Long-range forecasts tend to focus more on rain and sunshine than on wind direction, so you may have to search hard for wind information. Most marine forecasts stretch ahead for five days with a fair degree of accuracy, which should give you an idea of what to expect and whether there are any nasty systems forming that might generate more extreme winds. Examining these charts for a few days ahead of your cruise will help you to assess how the weather is developing and when the fronts and systems will be passing through. If you take your cruising seriously, it really does pay to get deeply involved in the weather so that you have a clear picture of the changes. However, a weather forecast is not cast in stone, even though the way weather charts are presented seem very positive. At best, it is an estimate of what the computer and forecaster think is going to happen and they constantly update the forecast as it gets closer to real time. There is a chapter in this book on the subject of weather because it is such a vital factor in cruising, but if you are seriously interested you could invest in one of the many dedicated weather books. The weather is both a fascinating and a frustrating science, and every time you think you have worked out what is going to happen, it will throw up a surprise – and the wind, on which you are relying for propulsion, can be a fickle mistress.

Getting to know the harbours

The Internet is a great source of weather information, but it has so much more of interest to the cruising man (and woman). Through Google Earth you can home in on pictures of the places you intend to visit to get an idea of what they look like as you enter harbour. You can get similar images on most electronic chart systems these days with graphic overlays, so there is no excuse for not knowing the layout of a strange harbour. Most harbours and marinas now have a website with information about berthing, contacts, refuelling and so on, but not all of this is kept up to date so remember to exercise a degree of caution. Even charts, both paper and electronic, are not necessarily up to date, so you will need your wits about you when entering a new harbour – but more on this later. Pilot guides are also a great source of information and can give a tantalising glimpse of what a place is like to visit, but generally their focus is more on the practical aspect of navigating into harbour and what you can find when you get there. Again, the very nature of a book means that it is never going to be fully up to date, but as a guide the pilot books are invaluable.

The sky can give you many clues about the weather to come.

Preparing the boat

When planning your cruise, you will of course need to focus on the boat itself. Take advantage of those long winter months to give it a good check over, because the most carefully planned cruise will be ruined if the boat is not reliable and something fails along the way. It is good practice always to check the boat before you go to sea, but over the winter that check can be much more intimate, delving down into the bilges and around the hidden corners of the engine room and inspecting all those parts you don't normally see. You are looking for any signs of deterioration or corrosion, particularly in relation to the many hoses and the electrical wiring on the engine and its auxiliaries, as well as the many bits and pieces that form the rigging and sails. In the days when I carried out yacht surveys, it was not unusual to find wear and tear in hidden places in the rigging that were not easily visible, and the winter is the time to look into all these details. Be sure to address any problems you find because they will never get better on their own and it is much easier to fix them in the boatyard or marina rather than out at sea, quite apart from the obvious risks involved in breaking down at sea. Hoses have always been my main concern because so many of the hoses around the engines and in the bilges are directly connected to the sea, so if a hose fails you have water coming into the boat. A routine replacement every few years is wise, and it is also a good discipline to compile a checklist and work your way through that. A cruise is so much more relaxed when you feel confident in the boat and its systems.

Margins for error

The reliability of the boat is important, but equally important when you are planning a cruise is to avoid pushing things to the limit. Always try to keep a margin in hand, whether it is the time to arrive in harbour before dark, the weather so that you are not operating close to what your boat in capable of and, perhaps most important of all, your experience so that you will have something left over to cope in the event of things going wrong.

Getting fuel and water can be important in your cruising plans.

Virtual cruising

There is a huge amount of information available to help you as you plan your summer cruises during the long winter nights. We have talked so far about doing the plotting and planning on the chart, but you will also want to know about refuelling and water possibilities, where you can get a meal or a drink ashore, possibly where the nearest service agent is for your engine, where you can find a berth, etc. Going back 30 years you would struggle to find much of this information, but today most of it is readily available on the Internet, in books, or even on your smartphone. From the comfort of your own home you can do virtual cruising and this can extend the pleasure of the cruise itself.

2

Planning your passage

Planning each leg of the cruise

We have looked at cruise planning and working out a general plan of how and where you want the cruise to go. Passage planning involves working out how and when you will get from leaving harbour in the morning to reaching your destination port that evening or overnight. It sounds so obvious to plan your passage before you go to sea, but it is surprising how many skippers think they will just head to such and such a harbour down the coast without making any detailed plans. To me, one of the pleasures of cruising lies in the planning of each leg – working out the best route, working out how to take advantage of the tides and currents, working out the sort of conditions to expect along the route, and looking forward with anticipation to arriving at the chosen destination. To spend a happy hour or two at the electronic chart plotter or over the paper chart is one of life's pleasures, and once you have done this you will have a much clearer idea of what lies ahead the next day.

Paper or electronic charts?

These days it seems old-fashioned to talk about paper charts when planning a passage but I still think they are the best option. Apart from the sheer pleasure of drawing lines on the chart and looking at the options, a paper chart offers a much wider view of the coastline and it may be possible to get the whole route onto one chart. With that view it is much easier to visualise the intended route and to get a clear picture in your mind.

Of course, you can also have the whole route displayed on an electronic chart, but the scale is so small on the limited area of the chart screen that it is difficult to visualise the detail. Indeed, the electronic chart is selective about what it shows, as you have to reduce the scale to get the whole route on display and it is possible for small islands and other features to disappear off the screen, although they will of course reappear when you expand the scale to look at the route in detail. With paper charts, every detail will be on display along the planned route, including all the main navigation marks.

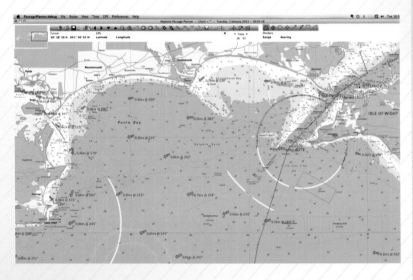

The electronic chart can give you all the information you need for passage planning but on a smaller scale display.

Another benefit of passage planning on a paper chart is that you will have a back-up should the electronic systems fail for any reason. Out at sea the electronic chart will be the focus of your navigation without doubt, mainly because it does all the work for you in terms of position plotting, but also because fewer yachts these days have space to lay out a paper chart at the helm. Unless you are one of the lucky ones who still have a dedicated navigation station, where there will also be room to consult the tide tables and pilot books, you will probably need to use the saloon table to lay out your paper chart.

The Global Positioning System (GPS)

'...The view from the cockpit is one of the most important tools in the navigator's repertoire.'

With passage planning, you need a beginning and an end to the voyage and for this you can pick a waypoint outside the departure harbour entrance and another at the entrance to the destination harbour. Now you need to think about the route in between, and this often involves setting safety margins such as the distance off headlands, any dangers along the route to be avoided, and buoys and other navigation lights that might be useful to give you a visual check. These visual checks are important; while GPS will give you an accurate position all the way along your route, I find I feel a lot more comfortable when I see a buoy where I expect it to be, which confirms that the GPS is working correctly. The problem with GPS is that it is so precise in the position it gives you that it doesn't allow any room for argument. However, there are some parts of the world where GPS is not reliable – there is one point off the coast of Italy, for example, where an aircraft beacon on a headland has such a strong signal that it stops the GPS working in that local area. Then there is always the risk that you may come up against GPS jamming. It seems crazy to think that someone would deliberately jam the vital GPS signal, but that is the way of the world today and you can buy jammers on the Internet for a few pounds, so there is a potential risk there.

The technology of the GPS system is one of the wonders of the modern world. By measuring the time difference of signals sent out from the satellites to the receiver on board, the computer can work out where you are, which is quite remarkable; but the signal that comes into the receiver is very, very weak, akin to the strength of a light bulb seen from hundreds of miles away, so it is not difficult to jam. However, let's not get gloomy about this aspect – just remember that GPS is wonderful for a navigator, but there is no guarantee it will work all the time. Even something as simple as a power failure or a low battery on board will stop the system working. Modern electronic systems for navigating are a great step forward and you need to embrace them and use them to their maximum capability; but in your passage planning always have at the back of your mind that the electronic positions may be unavailable just when you need them.

Visual indications

This is why any visual indications of your position can be a useful backup. You can get a pretty fair idea of where you when you are travelling along a coastline just by identifying the features on shore. There are plenty of clues there to indicate your position and they also give you something to focus on besides the screens. The view from the cockpit is still one of the most important tools in the navigator's repertoire and will also show you other vessels, for which you may have to take action to avoid.

GPS can tell you precisely where you are at any time.

Route planning on the electronic chart

1 Open up a chart that will show the beginning and end of the voyage on the same screen.

2 Remove any old routes or waypoints so you start with a clear display.

3 If you are offered a choice, select Rhumb Line from the Great Circle/Rhumb Line options.

4 Insert the start waypoint, zooming in to the chart to obtain a suitable scale that shows adequate detail.

5 Plot the en-route waypoints along the proposed course step by step around headlands and/or close to buoys, etc.

6 Plot the finish waypoint on a suitable scale of the chart.

7 Now go back to the departure waypoint and follow along the route at a large scale to ensure the route you have laid down does not pass close to or over any dangers.

8 Check that there is adequate distance off around the headlands.

9 Readjust the route as necessary, which you can usually do by 'rubber banding' – clicking on a waypoint and dragging it to a more suitable position.

10 When satisfied that the route is safe, save it to the plotter memory.

11 Check tidal information. Tidal flow can often be displayed on the electronic screen.

12 If you can, check for any updates for the charts in use and for any navigation warnings.

Safety margins

When plotting your route there is the temptation to pass close around headlands because you know precisely where you are with GPS. That is fine as long as everything is working well – but imagine a situation when the wind suddenly drops or perhaps you are not making much headway against a tide. These may not be particularly serious events as such, but they can be if you are close inshore, when you may not have the luxury of time to sort them out. In this case, what seems like quite a minor incident can escalate into something serious so my advice is, as a general rule, to play it safe and pass a reasonable distance offshore.

There can be exceptions to this rule, with some headlands offering a clear passage close inshore where there is a tidal race further out. Portland Bill is a prime example of this – to avoid the tide race, you need to pass the headland perhaps around 300 metres (330 yards) off the land. The option is to take the long way round, passing several miles off to avoid the area of breaking waves generated by the very strong tides here.

Deviating to shorten the distance between marks

Normally when you want to travel between two waypoints, you plot the direct line between the two to give the shortest distance. However, the shortest route may not be the best from a navigation point of view, and you want to look at other possibilities before finalising the route you take. Obviously you will check to ensure you are not proposing a route that takes you over or close to navigation hazards, but there can be other considerations to take into account.

If you are navigating using GPS position fixing on an electronic chart, the direct route should work because you are getting constant fixes along the way. However, it is always prudent to try to get checks about your position from sources other than GPS and you can do this by making minor modifications to your route. Look along your proposed route and seek out navigation marks on either side. These can be used as a useful visual position check and it may be sufficient just to be able to see them in the distance to get this check. However, look at the possibility of deviating from the straight-line course

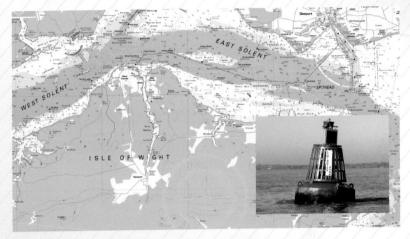

If you plan your route to pass close to buoys you can get a visual check on the position as well as see what the tide is doing.

if necessary, in order to pass closer to these marks (obviously checking that you will be passing on the safe side, away from the danger they mark). You could end up on something of a zigzag course but unless you have made major deviations the distance is not likely to be much greater. The benefit of adopting this tactic is that you should get regular visual checks about your position as you go along,

which are not only reassuring but also provide a check on the performance of the GPS. While this satellite system is very reliable and will rarely let you down, one of the golden rules of safe navigation is to try to get position checks from at least two sources. Making that deviation will do this in a very positive way, and could also allow you to get a check on what the tide is doing as you pass the buoy.

Whether you want to take this inshore passage under sail is up to you to decide; you might want to have the engine running, just in case. You find the same situation at other headlands, but passing close inshore is only viable if there are no off-lying rocks off the headland, such as you find at Lizard Point. This option requires a degree of local knowledge or experience, and while pilot guides and the chart give some indication of the possibilities, you might want to talk to other boaters or to local people before taking the inshore route.

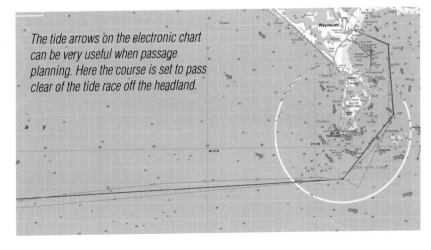

The tide arrows on the electronic chart can be very useful when passage planning. Here the course is set to pass clear of the tide race off the headland.

There are plenty of visual clues for navigation here.

Offsetting the course

It may seem logical to link up the departure and arrival points on the electronic chart when making a passage, but think ahead a little and consider the potential for problems. What might happen if the visibility closes in and you cannot see what you are looking for on arrival? If you are making a landfall on a featureless coastline, will you know which way to turn if you don't find land as expected?

With GPS position plotting these dilemmas should not pose a serious problem to navigation. However, should anything go amiss and you do not find what you expect when you reach the end of a passage, your next step may be to resort to guesswork – never a good solution. One way to avoid this dilemma is to build an offset into the course you steer. Rather than following the direct line between departure and arrival points, offset the course by, say, 5°. With this technique, you know you will arrive not at your chosen destination but to one side of it. However, because of the offset you will be certain which side you are on so you will know which way to turn. Offsetting the course is probably most useful when you are making for a harbour entrance with little in the way of distinguishing features until you get very close. The offset will allow you close to the coast and then to run along it to find the entrance.

However, this is a technique to be used selectively – finding a harbour where shallow water extends some way offshore, for example, could create more problems than it solves.

Tides

Tides can play a major part in your passage planning in northern waters – not so much the rise and fall of the tide, but the tidal currents generated by the water flowing to and fro along the coast. One of the joys of boating in the Mediterranean is that there is virtually no tide to worry about, so life and passage planning can be a lot simpler.

When you are in a yacht travelling at, say 5 knots, a 2 knot current will have a significant effect on progress and you will want to try to plan your passage to get maximum benefit from the tides. A tidal atlas showing the way the tides are running becomes an important part of your navigation repertoire, and this information is now built into many chart plotters.

With tidal flow it is not just the direction that is important but also the effect on the sea conditions. When the wind and tide are flowing in the same direction you will find a much more benign sea, with a longer wavelength, than when wind and tide are in opposition. When the two forces start to conflict and the wavelength is shortened this can result in steep waves, and even some breaking waves, depending on the wind strength. Portland Bill Race, for example, can become a maelstrom when the wind is against the tide, and you find the same effect off many headlands where the tidal stream tends to run faster because the water is forced into a narrower passage. When the wind is against the tide it may be a good idea to stay further off a headland, and you need to take this into account when carrying out your passage planning.

You need to know what the tide is doing as you head out to sea.

Distance on the electronic chart

Measuring distance on the paper chart is easy – with a pair of dividers, you measure off using the latitude scale at the side of the chart. Measuring distance on the electronic chart is not so simple, and it is also much harder to see at a glance what the distance might be off the land or other features.

Many electronic chart displays have a scale in the information bar at the top; but because you cannot transfer it to the chart you just have to measure by eye, which only gives a rough idea of the distance. Another option, found in the customising menu, is to display the latitude and longitude grid on the chart display. This enables you to work out the distance between the latitude lines and translate that into distance in the usual way.

A more positive measurement of distance can be made with the cursor. If you set this on the point to want to measure to, you will get a read-out of the distance and bearing from where you are. However, it only allows you to measure from the point where your boat is to the point of interest, and you cannot measure remote distances, such as setting a course and then seeing how far it passes off a headland. You can measure this by establishing waypoints and then looking at the distance between them, but this is cumbersome and time-consuming.

Range rings on the electronic chart would be a great idea but I believe the only way you can do this is by superimposing the radar display on top of the chart and using the radar range rings. When you know the intervals at which the rings are set, it is quite easy to make a visual judgement about remote distances. You should also be able to use the variable range marker in this way.

Perhaps now you can begin to see why passage planning is so important. With experience you will start to take all these factors into account mentally, but the best solution is still to write everything down – the courses and distances along the proposed route, the time and strength of the tidal streams, areas off headlands that might pose a challenge and, above all, the weather forecast. The latter is the most important aspect of passage planning because this will govern your judgement about whether it is safe to go to sea, whether you will face a pleasant comfortable cruise or be battling the waves for the whole way, and, of course, the directions in which you can sail.

A brief look at the weather

Weather forecasts are strange things. You would hope that weather forecasters offer a totally objective view of what the wind will be doing – its strength, and the direction from which it will be blowing. The direction is not much of a problem, although it is unlikely to be accurate to closer than 20 or 30°; but the strength presents a challenge. A forecaster always plays it safe when forecasting wind strength and gives a wind speed figure representing the strongest predicted wind instead of an average wind strength; so, with the exception of temporary gusts and increased local winds caused by land features such as valleys and high cliffs, the forecast wind will be the maximum you can expect to encounter.

So the easy part of passage planning is setting the courses you want to follow and the hard part can be assessing the likely sea conditions. By writing down the details of your planned passage you begin to see some logic in the process, and the information from the charts and pilot guides can be a great help. A recorded plan also means you will have enough information at hand to cope with the switch to visual or dead-reckoning navigation if the GPS lets you down.

Fuel requirements

Part of your passage planning should include fuel requirements. You will probably be planning to complete the voyage from harbour entrance to harbour entrance under sail, so you may only use fuel if you run a generator or the main engine for battery charging. However, knowing the distance you will be able to run with the available fuel on board can be useful information if you have to resort to using the engine, so this should also be part of your passage planning. Is there enough fuel on board to allow you to motor-sail part of the passage if you want to make the harbour earlier than planned? Never run your fuel margins so tight that you only have just enough fuel to make your chosen destination or an alternative closer harbour if the situation changes.

Nearly there…

Finally, it is useful to make a note, either on the paper chart or on your list of planning details, of the radio frequencies of the harbour and/or marina at your destination waypoint.

'…I love… the transformation from a static home in harbour to a lively craft…'

This long section on passage planning demonstrates just how much you need to take into account. It takes an hour or so to put the plan together, and I like to do this the night before so that when I want to get underway there are not so many distractions. All that will be outstanding then is to get the latest weather forecast and check around your boat before you leave, and then the big moment comes. I love this moment of departure when you undergo the transformation from a static home in harbour to a lively craft that you control and direct, and where you move from the constraints of the land into the freedom of the seas.

Trimming the sails as you leave harbour.

3

Leaving harbour

Shaking off the shackles of the shore

You've done all the planning and you can't wait to get started on your cruise. The temptation is strong just to jump on board, fire up the engine, assuming you are leaving harbour under power, and let go the ropes. But leaving harbour is a significant event – you are switching to an environment where to a certain extent you set the rules and regulations and you have a much greater degree of control and responsibility in terms of what can be done and where the limits are. If you are leaving from your home harbour and just going for a short run, you can probably get away with a fairly casual approach. If you are undertaking anything more serious, such as a longer cruise, then some planning and preparation is helpful before you set off. There is nothing worse than getting out to sea, only to have to stop and stow loose bits of gear, try to get some useful information out of the electronics, work out the navigation scenario, and prepare the boat for the sometimes lively waters. It is much easier to carry out those tasks in harbour before you leave.

Leaving harbour can affect skippers in different ways. For some, there is the sense of anticipation and excitement of heading off on a cruise to new waters. For others, there can be a sense of apprehension and responsibility as you enter the relative unknown of the open seas. Few skippers seem to really appreciate the changes that take place when you leave harbour and head out to sea – or, as the sailors of old used to say, 'shake off the shackles of the shore'.

Hoisting the jib on a classic cruiser.

That is quite an appropriate phrase, because in the marina you come under the influence of rules and regulations based on the demands of living on shore. You cannot pump out your bilges or, in some cases, your black and grey tanks. You have to lock up the boat when you go ashore and remember the code for the marina gate. You are restricted in the noise you can make because there are other yachts around. On the plus side, you can plug into the shore power so there is no need to run the generator, you probably have mobile phone and Internet reception, fresh water is readily available, and if something stops working on board, you can call on help to get it fixed. In short, in the marina you have most of the benefits of being on shore – but you also have all the rules, regulations and restrictions that go with them. *These* are the 'shackles of the shore' and they take many of the decisions about what you can do and when and how you do it out of your hands. The level of responsibility is relatively low.

Life on the ocean waves

When you head out into the open sea, all that changes. Of course you still have to comply with rules and regulations such as the COLREGs (see chapter 13), but it is you who sets the main pattern of life on board and the way the yacht is run and operated. It is you who has responsibility for the boat and its operation, and for the safety of those on board. You are responsible for the efficient running of the boat and for getting it to your destination.

With this change in responsibilities, leaving harbour should never be a casual event. Yes, you can take many aspects for granted, particularly when you are leaving your home harbour because you know the routines so well; but leaving from any other harbour or marina demands a degree of preparation and planning if you want things to go smoothly. As well as passage planning, you need to check out the boat and its systems and equipment, let someone know what your plans are, and – probably most important of all – you need to sort out and brief the crew. The crew can be your life support system out at sea if things take a turn for the worse, so engage them in the whole process so they know what is going on and what they can expect. Of course, you should still be able to get help from the shore or from other vessels if things do go badly wrong out at sea but it can be expensive, perhaps embarrassing, and at the very least spoil your pleasure, so a few moments spent checking things before you go can be both reassuring and reduce the chance of things going wrong.

Before you go

You can save so much aggravation when you are cruising from a bit of preparation. It is so much easier to secure something or to check something out when you are alongside in harbour than trying to do it out at sea when the boat may not provide the same sort of stable platform. You also want to have all the systems you might require for navigation up and running and ready for use BEFORE you go to sea. I have seen people scrabbling to get the radar or the electronic chart set up as they head out, when they should be concentrating on where they are going in the harbour channels. You see people suddenly having to rush around the boat when it hits the first of the swell out at sea and things on board start to crash or doors start to bang because they have not been secured properly. All it takes to avoid this is to spend 5 or 10 minutes preparing the boat for sea and you can leave harbour with a degree of confidence and security.

You take on more responsibility when you head out to sea.

'…You can save so much aggravation when you are cruising if you do a bit of preparation.'

If you go in and out of harbour frequently you will probably be in the habit of doing this more or less automatically – and if you are caught out once by not being prepared, you will learn from your mistakes and make sure it is done the next time. However, best of all is to have a plan so that nothing that should be checked and sorted before going to sea gets forgotten, and you can head out with confidence. I am a great believer in using checklists so that you tick off the items as you check the boat to make sure nothing important is overlooked.

Checklists

Four or five lists under different headings can be much more helpful than one long list. You might, for example, have one for the passage planning and navigation, one for the sails, one for the engines and systems, one for the boat, and perhaps a final one for things to do just before departure. By separating tasks in this way, you can tick off the boxes for passage planning when you have done this, perhaps the night before departure. You might want to do the engine and system checks some time before departure although some of these, such as checking that the seacocks and fuel valves are open or closed as appropriate, really ought to be done just before you leave.

The sample checklists included in this book will give you an idea of what to include. Each boat is different and you can adjust the lists to suit your own boat – you will know from experience what you need to add and what you can safely leave out. However, a checklist is only as good as the person using it and it is all too easy just to tick off the boxes without thoroughly carrying out the important physical checks.

Another important role for checklists is that to a certain extent they provide evidence that you checked things out before you went to sea. If you do find yourself in the unfortunate position of having an accident, your insurance company will be reassured to know that you were at least conscientious in your preparations.

Navigation

The navigation checklist is probably the most important of all in terms of complying with the passage-planning requirement. This list will cover the requirement to plot your intended route, check out the weather forecast, keep a list of the various VHF channels you might use, and, if you are travelling at night, a list of the navigation lights you might expect to see along the way. Tidal information is also important, both the expected heights and the direction of the tidal flow. You also want to consider alternative ports in case you have to cut short or extend your passage, and of course work out how far you are able to travel if you have to resort to using the engine. These are all the things you used to check before heading out to sea, but now you actually have to record them, which is a good discipline anyway.

Navigation preparation is even more important if you are cruising in a fast cruiser/ racer where it may not be possible to do much serious navigation planning when you are underway. The movement of this type of boat can make it difficult to plot routes and courses on a paper chart, and if the sea conditions are lively, you might even find it difficult to use the electronic systems owing to the movement of the yacht. One of the problems with navigation planning is that there are many options you might need to consider during a passage, such as alternative courses for improved sea conditions and alternative ports

This is the sort of problem that should be identified and fixed during the winter overhaul.

General checklist

✓ Fuel and water tanks topped up

✓ Engine and gearbox oil levels checked

✓ Engine water levels checked

✓ Steering working

✓ Radar on and set up, if you have one

✓ Electronic chart on and waypoints entered

✓ Paper charts available

✓ VHF radio on and working

✓ Portholes and hatches shut

✓ Loose equipment stowed

✓ Sail covers off and sails ready for hoisting

✓ Crew safety briefing

✓ Lifejackets on if required

✓ All ropes and fenders stowed after departure

you might want to use along the way. What happens if you do not make the boat speed you anticipated, and what about if the sea conditions deteriorate or the wind freshens more than forecast? You can spend some time looking at all the possible options, knowing you might only use perhaps 50 per cent of your navigation planning – the problem is that you do not know which 50 per cent you will use, so you prepare for all the alternatives. This is easier to say than to do, but it is a good discipline. We will look at navigation planning later in this chapter, but the box below gives an example of a checklist.

Sails

Checking the sails, ropes and rigging is easy to overlook – after all, they worked when you came into harbour, so why shouldn't they work when you leave again? However, at some point in their life, sails and ropes are going to chafe and wear out. You probably check them at the beginning or the end of the season and hope they will last. There is a good chance that they will – but it only wants a rope or sail to snag or lie awkwardly and chafe can set in very quickly, so a quick visual check does no harm before you leave. Particularly important is what is going on at the top of the mast, because you certainly don't want trouble up there when you are at sea. I use binoculars to look closely at the ropes and rigging there, in the hope that I will be able to spot any signs of trouble starting. I started doing this after having a forestay break on me in a fresh breeze off the west coast of Scotland because I had not noticed that the wire was beginning to fray close to where it entered the fitting at its attachment at the top of the mast. It decided to give up at 3 o'clock in the morning and we were lucky to save the mast by quick action in using a halyard to replace the forestay temporarily.

It does tend to be in the 'hidden' areas where trouble starts, and when I used to do survey work I found that many yachts had wear in the nip of the shackles and eyes of the fixed rigging where there was a constant small movement and bits of grit would get lodged there, triggering the wear process.

Using binoculars can help you to see any problems developing at the masthead.

Navigation checklist

✓ Waypoints entered and electronics programmed

✓ Radar on and set up to appropriate range

✓ Paper charts annotated and ready for use

✓ Departure electronic chart displayed and ready for use

✓ Echo sounder on and working

✓ VHF radio on and checked – set to harbour frequency

✓ Destination marina/harbour contacted

✓ Tide tables available and tidal streams considered

✓ Passage plan completed

✓ Distance under motor checked

✓ Weather forecast

✓ List of VHF channels

✓ Navigation lights on (at night or in fog)

You can only see this wear when the rigging is slacked off, and this is really one to check out at the beginning or end of a season, in the same way you would check out all the blocks and fittings. You can be sure that if something is going to fail in the rigging, it will do so at the most inconvenient moment, when it is under the heavier stress of adverse weather or conditions. Don't be too casual about a visual check of the standing and running rigging before you leave – on a quick check everything may look OK, but it is the detailed check that will find the problems.

It is not easy to give a sail and rigging checklist except to suggest you check that systems such as the roller reefing, if you have it, and the self-furling jib are working, that all ropes are running freely and ready for use, and that lead blocks are set to give a fair lead to the winches.

You need to slack off the rigging to check for any wear in the nip of the shackles.

Engine

For the engine checklist, include all those items you routinely check. Oil and water levels are the obvious ones, but a visual check around the engines is also a good plan. Look for anything amiss such as leaking pipes, loose fittings, and the state of the flexible drive belts and of any electrical wiring and connections you can see. Water leaks can often be detected by the telltale salt stains on the piping. Also check that any loose gear in the engine compartments is securely stowed because the last thing you want at sea is to have an oil drum or other equipment wandering around the engine compartment and causing damage. Check that the seacocks are open and the filters are clear. The flexible belt drive on the front of the engine that powers the water pumps and the alternator is a vital part of the engine and should be checked frequently for any sign of wear. If this belt fails, you lose your engine cooling and battery charging so it pays to follow the manufacturer's renewal regime.

Engine checklist

✓ Engine oil level checked

✓ Cooling water checked

✓ Spare oil on board

✓ Fuel filter checked

✓ Sea water intake filter checked

✓ Seacocks open

✓ Belt drive for the water pumps and alternator checked

✓ Battery and electrical switches in correct positions

✓ Loose equipment in the engine room and steering compartment stowed and secured

The battery stowage and connections should be checked for tightness at regular intervals.

The sea water intake filter needs checking to ensure it is clear.

Again, most of this will be routine and you may have carried out many of the checks when you came into harbour; but it does no harm to check again. While your intention is to make the passage under sail, it's likely that if you need to use the engine, you will need it in a hurry, so checking that everything is ready for a quick start will give you the reassurance that it will work when required. Space is often very restricted in modern sailboat engine compartments, which can make it difficult to see all the parts, but at least give it more than just a casual glance.

The boat

Take a quick walk around the boat and check each cabin to ensure that the portholes or windows are closed and that any loose gear brought out in harbour, including sunbeds and other cushions, has been carefully stowed. Ensure that locker doors, shower doors and cabin doors are closed so that they don't bang around at sea. The galley check is one of the most important. Make sure that the clip is on the fridge door to hold it shut, that everything is stowed away, that the gas (if you have it) is turned off, and that the fiddles are in place on the galley hob if you do plan to do any cooking underway. If you are expecting a lively passage where food preparation might be difficult, you might want to prepare some sandwiches and transfer hot drinks to a Thermos flask or two.

Items like this outboard motor stowage should be checked for security.

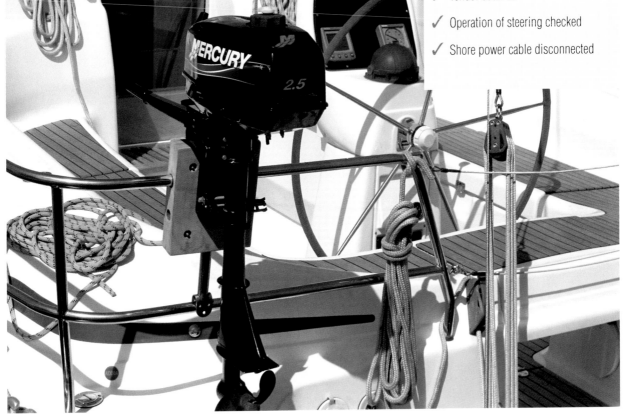

Boat checklist

✓ All hull windows and portholes shut

✓ All doors secured shut, including closet and shower doors

✓ Anchor secured if not in use

✓ Ropes and fenders stowed after departure

✓ All loose equipment secured in place

✓ Safety equipment available and ready for use, including the grab bag

✓ Fridge door secured shut

✓ Sunbed cushions removed and stowed if necessary

✓ Tender secured

✓ Operation of steering checked

✓ Shore power cable disconnected

Tenders

A tender can be both a help and a hindrance. It offers you a way to get ashore when you are at anchor or on a mooring, but can be difficult to stow and is possibly a liability if the weather turns nasty. Despite the problems, most cruising yachts have a tender and if you have a suitable type, you can use it to explore rivers and small harbours when the weather in the open sea stops you going out for the day.

There are two types of tender: the rigid tender, which has to be stowed in its full form (a small RIB or more conventional boat), and the inflatable tender, such as the Avon dinghy.

If your yacht is large enough, a tender garage is a good solution for stowing a rigid tender, although it might limit your choice in terms of size. The alternative is to stow the tender on the coachroof, provided you can launch and recover it from here and it does not obstruct the working of the yacht.

For most cruising yachts with no room to stow a rigid boat, an inflatable is the only option. It can be a pain having to inflate and deflate it every time you want to use it, and with their limited freeboard and limited power options they tend to be suitable only for harbour use.

An option, of course, is to tow the tender and if you are restricting your cruising to fine or moderate weather, this can work. However, towing the tender can be a liability and the tow rope can easily end up around the propeller. Also, it is easy to forget the presence of the tender until the moment when you want to go astern into a berth in a harbour.

If you are a marina cruiser, you can probably manage without a tender but for the more adventurous a tender can be an important piece of equipment, opening up many options that might otherwise be unavailable. In this case it is worth spending time sorting out both the best tender for your requirements and the best stowage option.

For the latter, good secure towing points are important, as is some means to prevent chafe on the tow rope. A reminder – hanging on the throttle lever can be a good idea so you are warned if or when you come to use the engine.

The tender can widen your cruising horizons but stowing or towing needs careful consideration.

Seacocks

The traditional school of thought is that you should turn off all the seacocks throughout the accommodation to prevent the possibility of any leaks through faulty piping. These days this is rarely done because the quality of the fixtures and fittings is much higher, and I feel it is more helpful to ensure that there is no faulty piping when you do your winter checks. By leaving the seacocks open you will then have toilets and sinks that you can use at sea, although these days most of the waste from these facilities is first taken to the grey or black water tanks. There are no formal rules at present about discharging grey waste water (water from showers and sinks) overboard, but it is suggested that you do not do this in harbours and marinas. Black water (waste from toilets) should be held in the holding tank and not discharged until you are at least 3 miles offshore. The reasoning behind closing seacocks is that, when they are open, the piping they serve is open to the full pressure of the water outside and this can be quite considerable when a yacht is bouncing around in waves, putting extra stress on the pipework.

The liferaft

If you normally have the liferaft stowed on deck when you are at sea, it is likely that you will stow it away or padlock it in place in harbour to prevent theft. In this case, it needs to be re-stowed or otherwise made ready for immediate use when you go to sea, and that padlock should definitely be removed. Also, don't secure it with a multitude of rope lashings, or you might be struggling if you ever have to use it.

Steering

Before you leave the berth, check that the steering is actually working. With the normal manual steering found on sailboats, such as the wire and pulley system or hand/hydraulics, it will be active all the time. You want to wind the wheel hard over to hard over and watch the response on the rudder indicator if you have one, or look over the stern if you can see the rudder from there, just to be sure that everything is free and working. Doing a similar check on the bow thruster is also a good idea so that you can be confident it will work when required. Just a flick on the lever or switch will tell you that you are getting the thrust you need, without affecting the boat much when it is tied up alongside. With wire and pulley steering you should add a check on the state of this to your checklist to ensure that the wires and other parts of the system are in sound condition. I once came across a yacht at sea that was on fire simply because the steering wire had broken and the wire had fallen onto the battery, where it shorted the terminals and started the fire!

Checking the radio

Check that all the electronics are switched on and working. This applies particularly to the VHF radio, which should be tuned in to the harbour or marina channel. A quick radio check with the harbour or marina control is a good idea, just to make sure the radio is working; and you may be obliged to call them anyway to get clearance from the harbour or marina authorities before you depart. After that it is best to put the radio on scan so it will pick up the distress, harbour and inter-ship frequencies without you having to switch manually. That way you will not miss anything important. A DSC VHF radio should pick up any message of importance to you anyway when you are at sea.

The departure checklist

This focus on checklists might seem excessive and, if you are experienced, most of them can be mental checklists because they are the sort of thing you do automatically. However, with the best will in the world you will probably forget something and it can be only when the boat starts to move around in waves that you find something is not secured, or perhaps you have forgotten to get the binoculars out ready for use. Most things you forget to do before actually leaving are not irrecoverable and they form part of the learning curve of going to sea but the checklists included here can hopefully serve as a reminder. Heading out to sea can be quite stressful because there is so much going on at the same time and the checklists will allow you to focus on where you are going and the feel of the boat, without having to sort out ropes and fenders that were not properly stowed. Then you will go to sea in a more relaxed and positive frame of mind.

A fifth checklist might be in order – the departure checklist. This can include a final check to ensure that anything moveable is securely stowed.

One thing you need to obtain before you go is the very latest weather forecast. There are so many sources these days that there should be no difficulty in getting good quality information. You will probably have access to the Internet when you are in harbour but not when you are out at sea, so it can be vital to get the latest weather information from this source.

An important safety point – does somebody know where you are heading, and when you expect to arrive? You can tell the Coastguard by radio, but friends or relatives might want to know as well.

It pays to look behind you when leaving harbour.

Everything has been checked and you can leave harbour with confidence.

If you are planning your cruise as a marina hopping exercise, you may have booked your next marina ahead of time. When you have made the decision to leave, a phone call to the marina to confirm departure is a good idea so they know to expect you. If you haven't made a booking, this is the moment to do it – most transient yachts leave a marina in the morning so a phone call at this time enables you to take advantage of vacant berths. If you leave it until you are well down the track, most or all of the available berths may have been snapped up and you will have to start searching. As always when you are cruising, it pays to think ahead.

Depending on the sea conditions when you leave harbour, the movement of the boat may make it difficult to do any food preparation or to make hot drinks. Preparing these before you leave ensures that you have food and drink on the passage and these can be a great morale booster in lively seas. You know things can't be so bad if you can still serve hot drinks, and a Thermos flask should be an essential piece of the boat's equipment. Also think about putting on waterproofs before you leave because trying to put them on at sea can be quite challenging and distracting.

As a last thought, make sure you take a seasickness pill before you go if you are afflicted. I have been prone to seasickness all my sea-going life and these pills are a lifesaver. Make sure the crew take them as well if they need them, because seasick crew can be a considerable liability.

Briefing the crew

You are officially obliged to give your crew a briefing to meet safety requirements, telling them where the lifejackets are stowed, where the liferaft is and how to use it, what to do in the event of an emergency, and what not to do when they are on board. In addition, you should add details of where the cruise will be going that day and how it will be organised – who will be keeping watches and when, for example, and what sort of food and drink will be available. It is so easy to take all these things for granted and expect people to know

Crew checklist

✓ Crew briefing carried out

✓ Suitable clothing being worn

✓ Lifejackets on?

✓ Seasickness tablets?

✓ Duties allocated

✓ Food and drink prepared

what they are doing; but it does no harm to spell it out in some detail. If you have a regular crew, the briefing can be very short and sweet, but with newcomers it needs to cover a wide spectrum of topics. The briefing is even more important if there are children on board and they should be told in considerable detail what to do and not to do.

Lifejackets
Among the safety aspects, the issue of whether or not to wear lifejackets can be a contentious one. The authorities say you should always wear one when you go to sea, and in a small open boat that makes sense. There is a lot to be said for wearing one when you are sitting in the cockpit even in fine weather, because even the best of us can slip up and there may be a sudden demand to go onto the foredeck. However, if you are inside in the comfort of a saloon, you could dispense with the lifejacket but make it a rule that one should be put on if you go outside for any reason. Certainly anybody on board who is showing signs of seasickness should always wear a lifejacket because they tend not to have the same sense of survival as a fully fit person. The other ones to watch are the smokers, who these days will normally stand aft to smoke, where they could be more vulnerable.

The only good lifejacket is one with a crotch strap. In the water you are suspended from the lifejacket and without a crotch strap the lifejacket can ride up and not provide the correct flotation, so this feature is essential. If you wear a lifejacket, make sure you wear it correctly with straps tightened, so it can do its job should the need arise.

Lifelines are also a great safety feature and while the requirement for these in the cockpit may be a question of choice, they should certainly be a must when on the foredeck. In winds of over, say, force 4, they can be a good idea in the cockpit as well. These days harnesses for lifelines and lifejackets are usually combined so you have the full safety package in one piece, but there is still the requirement to actually clip on. As they say, a lifejacket will not work if it is not worn – and a lifeline will not work if it is not clipped on.

Watch keeping
The question of watch keeping can be quite casual if the voyage is just a day trip and you as skipper will be around to keep a close watch on progress. On longer voyages, particularly overnight trips, a more formal watch system is required as people will want to sleep, so you will need to look at who among the crew has the experience to keep a watch on their own so you can sleep soundly without worry. These factors should be settled before you leave and the briefing is the place to do it so that everyone on board is in the picture. If the sea conditions are likely to be lively, a few words about keeping secure on board and finding a secure place to sit or stand will not come amiss, because the last thing you want is for one of the crew to be thrown across the boat and injured.

Leaving from a marina berth

In most cases, getting out of a marina berth is quite straightforward provided you have gone in stern first as is normal. With the mooring systems found in most Mediterranean harbours you are always stern-to, but you have a bow anchor rope that you have to get rid of as you let go aft and move forward. The biggest risk when leaving is getting a rope around your propeller, so move cautiously in the early stages until you can be sure all the ropes have sunk or been taken on board. When moored stern-to in a finger pontoon berth, all you have to do is cast off the ropes.

Top Tip

Watch your stern

Depending on the type of boat you are using and its keel shape, you will find that it pivots at a point somewhere near the geometrical centre of the keel when manoeuvring and you need to allow for this, particularly when leaving a berth.

It seems logical that as you come out from a marina berth and see the finger pier passing astern, you turn the helm to get clear. However, that pivot point means that when you turn the helm the bow goes the way you want, but the stern will also swing out, in the opposite direction. So if you turn too quickly on leaving, your stern could easily make contact with the boat or quay alongside. The answer is not to make the turn until you are clear of the berth on both sides, which can be easier said than done – so many marinas these days are so tight on space that you have very little room to manoeuvre as you leave the berth. However, if you managed to get in you should be able to get out – but don't make that turn too quickly.

Dress for sea when doing your final checks before leaving.

You need to watch your stern as you move out of this marina berth.

In most marina berths you need to move ahead in a straight line until the stern is clear before turning along the channel. There are two situations when the departure can be more complex – one where there is a tide or river current running through the marina, and the other when there is a fresh wind blowing. In both these cases there may be a considerable sideways movement when you let go of the ropes and you will need to compensate for this with the bow thruster, if you have one, or with the steering. If you are faced with this situation as you leave the berth, moving away quickly can reduce the sideways movement and get you into the open water. Sailboats usually steer very quickly even at low speed, so you should have good control.

Leaving from a quay

Leaving from a quay or jetty berth can be a bit more complicated because you have to move the boat sideways out from the quay. If you have a bow thruster this is easy, and if there is a tide or current running you can use this to help you edge out, using the engine to hold the boat and the steering to ease the boat away from the quay. In still water it can be more challenging because the stern will swing in if you try to angle the bow out. Manoeuvring a boat within the tight confines of a harbour means working out the various forces acting on the boat, such as the wind and the tide, and then using controls such as the engine, steering and thruster to counteract these forces and get the boat to move in the direction you want.

Using 'springs'

When you tie up your boat you will have the bow and stern lines out, but for good mooring practice you will also put out springs. These are ropes leading from the bow aft and from the stern forward and their main use is to help keep the boat alongside without binding it in tightly, as would happen with just the bow and stern ropes. However, another use is 'springing' the boat off – hence the name.

☑ Top Tip

Springing into a marina berth

These days, with bow thrusters, 'springing off' may be a lost art; but without a thruster a spring can be used to swing the bow or the stern out to help you get away from a tight mooring. It works like this – if you want to swing the stern out, rig the forward spring line from a point close to the bow, let go of everything else, and then gently nudge the boat ahead, using the engine if you have a choice. As the engine thrust takes effect and the rope tightens, the stern will swing out against the pull forward and you can get the boat at an angle of maybe 45° to the quay.

You will need good fendering between the boat and the quay at the bow and it is sensible to have the spring rope on a bight so that you can let one end go from on board and then pull the other end in without any need to have a person on the shore.

Above left: A bit of planning can help you navigate your way out of a complex harbour channel.

Above right: Visual navigation will normally work well when leaving harbour.

The fenders should be stowed as you leave.

Navigating a harbour channel

Once away from the berth or out of the marina, your next challenge is to navigate the harbour channels. This can be a long and winding trip or just a short dash to deep water; either way, you need concentration. Going out to sea always seems easier than coming in because you tend to be heading out into more open water all the time, making navigation simpler. Every harbour entrance channel is different and if you are not familiar with the one you are using, some preparation beforehand is necessary because the changes can come up thick and fast. Once again, a paper chart can be a great guide to what to expect in the entrance channel but the electronic chart, with its automatic plotting, can also help considerably. The GPS plot of the electronic chart is normally reasonably accurate but please don't rely on it 100 per cent – a visual check as you pass buoys and other marks is vital. At night it is much trickier because you have to count light flashes on the buoys in order to identify each one, and it can also be much harder to judge distances. Leaving harbour is largely a matter of visual navigation and you need to be prepared for this. In fog you probably should not be leaving harbour anyway, but the aspects of fog and night navigation are covered in a later chapter.

To leave or not to leave?

There will inevitably be times when you are faced with decisions about whether the conditions are right to leave harbour or whether you should hold fire and wait for improvements. Most of these decisions will be weather-related, although your pre-departure check through the boat may throw up a problem that will force a decision about whether to go or to stay and fix the problem. Weather-related decisions will be based on the weather forecast the night before departure and you may simply decide not to go because the forecast looks so bad.

If the forecast is uncertain, you can put off any decision until the morning of departure and see what the forecast looks like then. This is your second cut-off point for departure and with a good forecast there is no problem, you go. It is those awful in-between forecasts that give you pause for thought.

In this situation there are many factors to consider. How capable are the crew to cope with adverse conditions? Are there critical points along the proposed route, such as a headland

Too little wind can also be a problem but there are promising signs on the horizon.

Lifeboat men never turn back

I once left Rosslare in Ireland in a lifeboat and we were on passage to round Land's End and then on up the English Channel. The forecast was horrific, north-westerly force 10, but in a lifeboat you are expected to go out in these conditions and on this occasion we were evaluating a new design so there was a double reason to keep to the schedule. I had second thoughts about it when we got out to the Tusker Rock Lighthouse and found a huge sea running. Logic was strongly in favour of turning back and there would have been no disgrace in doing so, but I gave it a bit longer and found the seas lost some of their violence in more open water; the boat and crew got into the rhythm and we kept going. Later, when we tied up after one of the most exciting voyages of my life, I voiced my misgivings to the crew and said I had thought about turning back. Back came the reply, 'If you had done that, Sir, you would not have had a crew. Cromer lifeboat men never turn back.'

Lifeboatmen may have a tradition of never turning back when they are going out on a rescue, but in ordinary boating there is no disgrace and it can be the sensible option.

where the seas could be more threatening? Is the wind forecast to increase or decrease? Is the forecaster being pessimistic and perhaps adding extra wind strength to make sure that all possibilities are covered? What are the capabilities of the boat and crew to cope with adverse conditions? In adverse conditions you might make slower progress than you expected – will this affect your arrival time in daylight? What will the conditions be like in the entrance of the arrival port?

There can be some clues to help you with this difficult decision. Is the wind strength increasing or decreasing? If it is increasing, there is every chance that the worst of the weather is still to come; but if it is decreasing, the forecast is possibly telling you what you have just had rather than what is to come. Check to see which way the weather systems are moving for a guide to the likely conditions where you are. A check with Coastguard stations or harbours along the route might give you some indication but take reports from these sources with a pinch of salt. To get a good view, Coastguard or Coastwatch stations are usually mounted high, where the wind can be quite a bit stronger than at sea level; also, such authorities will always advise caution to cover themselves. The decision is ultimately yours and yours alone and the easiest option is to stay put, gather all the information you can, and then weigh things up carefully.

You can put off your decision for a while and go out and have a look at the conditions outside the harbour, where you will get a much better feel for what it is like and how your boat is coping. I have done this many times and found to my surprise that things are fine when you get outside and nothing like as bad as you imagined.

The clouds can give clues about what the weather might hold in store.

Any port in a storm

In your passage planning you will have looked at the availability of alternative ports along the route in case you want or need to cut your voyage short. One of these alternatives is the port you have just left – you always have the option of turning round and heading back if you don't like what you see when you get outside. It is rather like the safety briefing on an aeroplane: 'There are six emergency exits on this aircraft and remember that the nearest one may be the one behind you.' In the case of cruising, the nearest and possibly the best alternative port could well be the one you have just left. It probably seems obvious when you see it in writing, but how many passage planners even think about that port as a refuge or as one of the alternatives that is always open?

The trouble when you are making a passage is that your focus is always on where you are going, not where you have come from. If conditions deteriorate or you come up against a problem, you don't feel too bad about turning off to one side to a nearby port to find shelter – but turning back? No, that is not an option. It feels like giving in and perhaps questions your judgement about going out in the first place. Of course, a lot depends on how far you have travelled down your route and what alternative ports are on offer; but the port you have left will at least have the benefit of being familiar territory. You should have no problem in finding your way back into harbour safely, even under adverse conditions, and that can be a major bonus compared to entering an unfamiliar port.

Heading out to sea in a breeze.

'…You don't want to be fighting the wind and the waves.'

The sails should be chosen to match the forecast weather.

Trusting your own judgement

A recent shipping forecast went out saying the wind would be force 5 to 7 and, locally, gale force 8. The inshore waters forecast was more pessimistic, warning of gales or severe gales. Talk about hedging your bets – those two forecasts issued at the same time were giving wind strengths that could vary from a feasible 17 knots of wind to an untenable 45 knots. In force 5 there was a good possibility of making the 20-mile passage along the coast. In the force 8 of a gale or force 9 of a severe gale, there was no sensible chance.

As far as I was concerned, the only solution was to go out and have a look. It can be really difficult to tell what the wind is doing when you are in harbour, so going outside gives a much better indication of the wind strength and, more importantly, the sea conditions. It was quite lively in the harbour entrance, which is what you might expect with an onshore wind; but once through that, the seas flattened out, and within a couple of hours we were safely tied up, secure in the knowledge that we had backed our judgement rather than listened to the pessimism of the weather forecaster. The one proviso of the whole operation was that, once outside, we would turn back if we did not like what we saw.

It is so easy when you go to sea these days to rely on other people's judgement rather than your own. You tend to take weather forecasts as gospel, thinking that in this modern computer age they must be right and if they say it is going to be bad, then it will be. You have to remember that the forecast is just that, a forecast – and when you look at that forecast I mentioned above, you can see that there must have been considerable doubt in the forecaster's mind, otherwise why offer such a range of wind strengths? You might have an intelligent guess at what it is going to be like outside but in my mind there is only one way to be sure – go out and have a look, on the proviso that you can turn back if you don't like what you see.

Putting in a reef

When the forecast conditions are like this, you also have to consider whether to put in a reef or two before you go. I know there are cruising people who say that if you are thinking about putting in a reef, then don't go. Most yachts are quite happy sailing with a reef down and the prospect of reefing should not necessarily deter you from going to sea. A lot will depend on the strength of the crew, but reefing can be a sensible precaution. It is much easier to put one in before you leave than to do it at sea, and you can always shake it out when you are out there. The same applies to putting up any sail when you are still in harbour, and it is pretty well standard practice these days to put the main up just after you have left your berth, when working on the foredeck is a lot safer. With modern roller foresails it is easy to deploy these when you come to switch off the engine and take up sailing. The point at which you do this depends a great deal of the type of harbour you are leaving – progress under sail alone is best commenced when there is adequate sea room, but again that is your choice.

Negotiating with the weather and making decisions about it in this way is one of the skills you should develop as a boater and we look at this in much more detail in a later chapter. You don't want to be fighting the wind and the waves because in any battle like that the sea is always likely to win – and, let's face it, you are out there on a pleasure cruise! Having said that, you can gain a lot of satisfaction from making judgements about the best course of action and finding seamanlike solutions to cruising problems.

Prayer is no substitute for preparation.

Ready in all respects for sea.

4

Assessing weather
and sea conditions

The most critical aspect of cruising

The weather plays such an important part in any cruising planning and execution in Northern Europe that it is worth a whole chapter. Understand the weather and you can get much more pleasure and satisfaction out of cruising. I qualify the weather for Northern Europe because here it is largely dictated by the jet stream, a funnel of air high up in the sky that takes a constantly changing course around the world, with its average line located perhaps around 40° north in the winter and further north in the summer. The reason the jet stream has such an influence is that it marks the border between the two opposing weather patterns that dominate the world's weather, and where these two meet is an area of considerable turbulence, which tends to dictate the weather we experience. Head down to the Mediterranean and, in the summer months at least, you'll escape much of this turbulence, which is why the weather there tends to be much more settled and predictable. It is not hard to see why many boaters seek out this location for cruising; but it lacks the challenge and variety of the cruising conditions in more northern waters.

Cloud patterns can give you a clue about the weather timing.

The weather and the associated sea conditions are probably the most critical aspect of cruising. Understanding the weather and sea conditions and how they can develop and change will help you to assess what you can achieve when cruising. In this chapter we will look at how to get the good-quality weather information mentioned earlier; but that is only half the battle. First of all, you need to be able to interpret what the weather forecast is saying and translate this into an assessment of the sort of weather you will actually encounter where you are. Remember that weather forecasts are only that – a forecast; they tend to be very general in nature and you can get a much more precise idea of what your weather will be like if you fine-tune the forecast to your requirements. Once you understand how forecasts are prepared and how the weather develops, you will be more aware of what is going on and, more importantly, what is likely to happen in the future.

Questioning the forecast

Weather forecasts generally sound very certain, and this is particularly the case with radio and TV forecasts and those issued over the Navtex system, which tend to focus on your particular area rather than giving a more general picture of the weather. However, it is worth questioning the accuracy of the forecast if you want the most reliable information possible.

You can often assess the reliability of a forecast by looking at how many variable factors are included. A forecast that predicts 'winds force 4 to 5, perhaps force 6' should suggest that either the forecaster is not entirely sure about what is going to happen or he thinks that wind strengths will differ throughout the forecast area. The difference in the wind strengths from the lowest to the highest in such a forecast could mean a virtual doubling of the wind strength over the range that the forecast covers. The same applies when there is a degree of vagueness about the wind direction of anything up to 90° or even more.

Forecasters may also mention changes that are going to occur in the weather 'later'. Does 'later' mean in a few hours' time or a day later? This apparent vagueness as to the various weather factors can make it very difficult to decide on whether or not to go to sea and you will probably take the cautious decision and stay in harbour.

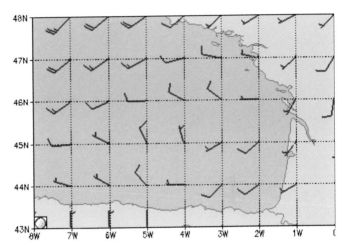

This wind chart promises fine weather across the Bay of Biscay.

However, you can get a clearer picture if you carefully study the options being offered. You need to remember that the forecaster will often be hampered in giving a precise forecast because it has to cover a wide area of sea. Weather can change considerably over the 200 or 300 miles encompassed by a single forecast sea area and the forecaster has to cater for all parts of the region in one compact forecast.

You can help to resolve matters by knowing where you are within the forecast sea area and having a better understanding of what is going on. If, for example, the weather patterns are moving from west to east and you are in the western part of the sea area, then you know you will experience any forecast changes early on. In the east the change will come later. I can recollect a storm that was forecast for every sea area on the English Channel and it was taking place in the far west, while the conditions in the Dover area were still fine, although likely to deteriorate. Having access to weather maps can be of great help in developing your understanding of the weather forecast, as you can then see how the weather is actually developing and moving. Local signs and conditions can also remove some of the question marks.

When you are using weather maps for your forecast, there is less scope for questioning. The map presentation tends to be much more precise and shows aspects like wind strength and direction in a more local way. However, these weather maps will not generally take account of local conditions such as the effects of the land, the tides and the shallows, so you can still add your own interpretation.

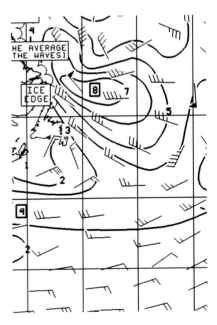

Wind arrows showing strong winds in the North Atlantic around a depression.

Left: These clouds suggest a squall passing through.

Working with the wind

You need to translate the wind strengths given in the forecast into the sort of sea conditions you can expect on your cruise. The sea conditions may be a secondary consideration in a sailboat but they can affect comfort levels considerably. Translating wind strength into sea conditions is not easy because there can be so many variable factors, and while you might find forecasts of wave height and period for the open ocean areas of the sea, you are very unlikely to find them for the inshore waters where you will mainly operate.

When you are cruising, the weather and sea conditions will dictate what you can and can't do. In an ideal cruising world the sea would always be calm, with a great sailing breeze and the sun shining; but in reality days like that are few and far between in northern waters and are a real bonus when you find them. In reality the weather will be constantly changing – sometimes good, sometimes bad – and one of your main jobs as a skipper is to assess the conditions and decide whether they are suitable for what you propose to do. On days when the conditions are fine, the decision will be easy; but when the weather appears to be marginal, you have to decide whether to stay in port and wait for the adverse weather to pass through or head out to sea and hope you can cope. To make a reasoned decision, you need an understanding of how the weather is created, how it behaves and how it is forecast.

Negotiating with the weather

It is also important when cruising to learn how you can 'negotiate' with the weather. You might think there is no scope for negotiation because you cannot change the weather itself. However, your negotiating power comes from the effect of the wind on sea conditions and you being able to operate your yacht on different courses with different sail settings. Quite a few aspects of progress are under your control and it is these that allow you to negotiate with the weather; for example, you can alter the timing of your progress, and possibly get shelter from the land. Then there is the weather itself – a moving and changing event, usually fast moving in adverse conditions and slower moving or even static when conditions are fine. While you cannot do anything to influence the weather, understanding how it is moving and changing can strengthen your negotiating position, with timing being one of the variable factors.

The time factor

'...the weather and sea conditions will dictate what you can and can't do.'

Very active clouds promise wild winds.

You can exercise considerable control over the weather you experience because it will change with time, sometimes quite rapidly. Using the factor of time in this way may result in delaying your departure for a day or so, but even delaying by an hour or two can allow a front to pass through your position, producing a significant change in the weather you experience, such as a change in wind direction and strength, which you can use to your advantage.

There can often be lulls in wind strength, allowing you to complete a short passage before the strong winds return; and it helps to be able to identify this possibility. Another possibility is to alter your direction of travel so that you benefit from improved wind and sea conditions to maximise the sailing potential of your yacht.

In order to negotiate with the weather, you will need the best possible weather information you can obtain, relating as far as possible to your location.

Of particular importance is the timing of weather changes that are forecast to occur. You will need to relate these to your current position, and local observations such as rain density and cloud types can often provide you with an indication of impending change. Local topography and tides can also have an effect on the sea conditions, and it is up to you to weigh up all the factors involved in the weather equation that may affect you.

The more information you have (and the better the quality of the information), the stronger will be your negotiating position and this could mean the difference between a day spent at sea and a day spent in harbour.

You may be able to put a more accurate timing to the forecast by studying the cloud patterns.

Do not rely too much on weather reports from coast stations high above the sea.

The nature of forecasting

You might ask why the forecast does not do the work for you and give a precise summary of what the conditions will be like in your area. A personal weather forecaster who knows your position and your intentions will give you the dedicated information you want; but you have to pay a lot of money for that level of forecasting. If the forecasting service you are using comes free, it will almost certainly be a general forecast for the area without any precise timing of changes.

You also need to remember that forecasts tend to focus on wind strengths rather than sea conditions. Wave and swell forecasts are available for open sea areas but not for inshore waters. Forecasts of conditions in inshore waters can involve several other factors in addition to the wind strength and direction, and with some of these factors being changeable even within a mile or two, the forecaster's job becomes very difficult within the context of a precise forecast. The forecaster has to cover himself and if he says that the waves will be, say, 2m (6ft) high in a particular region, but there could possibly be waves of 3 or even 4m (10–13ft) high lurking within that region, he is in trouble. So the precise sea and swell conditions that would be so helpful when planning what to do the next day are not available from official forecasting sources.

However, it is possible to make your own forecast of what you might expect along your proposed route once you grasp the basics of how the wind, sea and other influences interact to create waves. It can be a complex process, but with experience you should be able to make a pretty good forecast.

To help understand the situation let us look at how the professionals develop their weather forecasts. A hundred years ago, when there were little or no means of communicating over long distances, forecasts were made by looking at the skies, and understanding how they were developing and what the changes indicated. Barometer readings were also a valuable forecasting tool, particularly in terms of whether the barometer was rising or falling, and the speed. Barometer changes could indicate the approach of high- or low-pressure areas that would change the weather conditions. Even so, sailors would set out to sea with only a very limited knowledge of what was in store for them.

It makes you realise what heroes some of those early sailors must have been, with so little knowledge of what lay in store for them; today, however, with worldwide communications shuttling weather information around the world, we have a much better handle on the weather and its changes. These days, detailed weather information is fed into some of the most powerful computers in the world, in which is stored detailed data about the weather from as far back as records exist, so that when the current weather data is processed and analysed it can be compared to the historical records, allowing a matching scenario to be identified. From that, the computer can see what happened last time and make the assumption that much the same thing will happen again. Complex fluid dynamics are thrown into the pot to enhance the forecast accuracy.

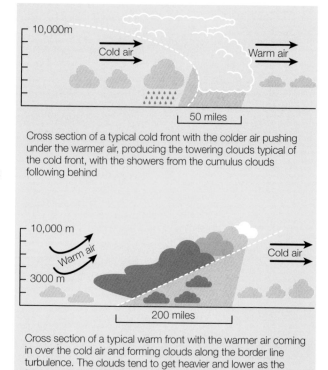

Cross section of a typical cold front with the colder air pushing under the warmer air, producing the towering clouds typical of the cold front, with the showers from the cumulus clouds following behind

Cross section of a typical warm front with the warmer air coming in over the cold air and forming clouds along the border line turbulence. The clouds tend to get heavier and lower as the front nears sea level and the rain starts with the heavier cloud

Below: The traditional synoptic weather chart has a lot of information but you need to understand the codes to decipher it.

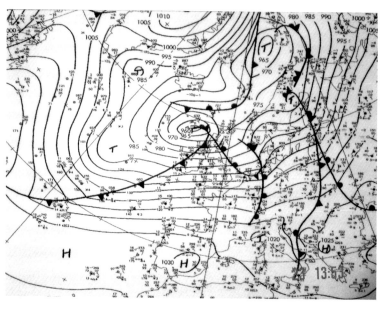

Marine forecasts glossary

Gale warnings

Gale – Winds of at least Beaufort force 8 (34-40 knots) or gusts reaching 43–51 knots

Severe gale – Winds of force 9 (41–47 knots) or gusts reaching 52–60 knots

Storm – Winds of force 10 (48–55 knots) or gusts reaching 61–68 knots

Violent storm – Winds of force 11 (56–63 knots) or gusts of 69 knots or more

Hurricane force – Winds of force 12 (64 knots or more)

Note: The term used is 'hurricane force'; the term 'hurricane' on its own means a true tropical cyclone, not experienced in European waters.

Timings

Imminent – Expected within 6 hours of time of issue

Soon – Expected within 6–12 hours of time of issue

Later – Expected more than 12 hours from time of issue

Movement of pressure systems

Slowly – Moving at less than 15 knots

Steadily – Moving at 15–25 knots

Rather quickly – Moving at 25–35 knots

Rapidly – Moving at 35–45 knots

Very rapidly – Moving at more than 45 knots

Visibility

Fog – Visibility less than 1,000 metres (1,100 yards)

Poor – Visibility between 1,000 metres (1,100 yards) and 2 nautical miles

Moderate – Visibility between 2 and 5 nautical miles

Good – Visibility more than 5 nautical miles

Pressure tendency in station reports

Rising (or falling) slowly – Pressure change of 0.1–1.5 hPa in the preceding 3 hours

Rising (or falling) – Pressure change of 1.6–3.5 hPa in the preceding 3 hours

Rising (or falling) quickly – Pressure change of 3.6–6.0 hPa in the preceding 3 hours

Rising (or falling) very rapidly Pressure change of more than 6.0 hPa in the preceding 3 hours

Now rising (or falling) – Pressure has been falling (rising) or steady in the preceding 3 hours, but at the time of observation was definitely rising (falling)

Note: For those more familiar with the millibar, 1 hPa = 1 mb

Wind

Wind direction – Indicates the direction from which the wind is blowing

Becoming cyclonic – Indicates that there will be considerable change in wind direction across the path of a depression within the forecast area

Veering – The changing of the wind direction clockwise, e.g. SW to W

Backing – The changing of the wind in the opposite direction to veering (anticlockwise), e.g. SE to NE

This computer-generated forecast is then checked and possibly modified by a human forecaster, who may tune out any idiosyncrasies, and there you have the basic information for the forecast in the form of a pressure chart. You have to remember that the weather operates in four dimensions, including time, and what happens high up in the atmosphere can also affect what happens near sea level. It is a hugely complex situation that changes by the minute and the forecasters do a great job in making sense of it all. In recent times, satellite pictures of the weather have been added to the available information sources, but these striking images only show the past or current weather.

This brief explanation should help you to understand why the weather forecasts do not always get it right. They can be remarkably accurate, and provide the best information available about the weather, but in many cases the weakness in the forecast can be in the timing. Trying to assess how fast areas of low pressure and their associated fronts are going to travel is difficult – so there is every chance you will get the winds that are forecast, but not exactly on cue; and this is where your local observations can help.

Weather forecasts on the Internet

Most of us today rely on broadcast radio weather forecasts or on what we can find on the Internet. Many harbour and marina offices put up a printout of the weather maps for a day or two ahead, but these will be very similar to what you can find on the Internet. Weather maps on the Internet are quite amazing in the level of information available, with forecast maps showing the predicted situation for up to five days ahead. Land forecasts look even further ahead, but at five days you tend to be reaching the limits of forecast credibility.

Useful websites

The following websites provide weather maps and information for up to five days ahead and are a wonderful free source of weather information when planning a cruise. Remember that there is no guarantee the weather will turn out as forecast and when you start looking more than three days ahead you may find that different websites give conflicting information.

www.weathercharts.org
This site gives a long list of websites where you can access a huge variety of weather information, ranging from the conventional black and white weather charts to colourful charts that show wind, waves and swell conditions for up to five days ahead, and even information about snow coverage in Antarctica and volcanic eruptions. Many of the charts can be programmed to operate on a loop showing a moving picture of how the weather is developing over a five-day period. From the very wide selection on

offer, you can find the ones that fit your requirements and take it from there. I love the traditional black and white charts that show the weather fronts and the isobars, but you have to interpret these to see what the weather will be like.

This site also gives a variety of satellite charts, where you can see what has happened over the past 24 hours or more (but not what is going to happen). Another feature of this website is that you are directed to websites with the tidal predictions for around the world.

www.passageweather.com
This is a great website dedicated to marine forecasts for up to seven days ahead. Here you can get very specific weather charts to fit your requirements and I have used this one a lot. You can also download Passage Weather as an App on your iPhone or iPad – so as long as you are within 3G coverage you can get up-to-date forecasts from this source.

www.bbc.co.uk/weather/coast
There are some good weather charts here from the British Met Office, showing the isobars and main frontal systems for up to five days ahead for Northern Europe, plus other marine-related weather information.

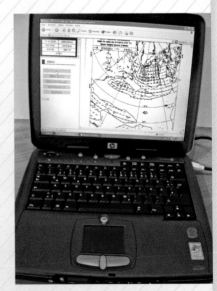

There is a huge amount of weather information on the Internet.

Using satellite information

Pictures from satellites have become a new tool for forecasters and it is now possible for yachtsmen to download satellite pictures. These provide a view from 200 miles above of what the weather is doing on the surface of the earth; but while they can be a valuable tool for forecasting, these images do have limitations.

The biggest limitation is that while the satellite picture shows the swirling clouds of a low-pressure area and measures the progress of the weather, the images are not forecasts and only show the current weather. To a forecaster this can provide valuable information for predicting the future; but the yachtsman out at sea is already experiencing the weather conditions. So for all their good looks and wonderful technology, satellite images do not present an eye into the future and their main value lies in being able to see the extent of the weather.

Satellite pictures come in a variety of formats but of most interest are those taken using visible light. These show the extent of the cloud cover, which can be a good indication of what is going on below. Knowing your own position on the satellite picture, you can see where you are in relation to the moving weather and get a better idea of when to expect changes.

You could, for example, see the typical cloud cover of a warm front lying out to the west of your position. From this you should be able to estimate when you will start seeing the first signs of the front arriving. Alternatively, if you are in the frontal zone already you should be able to get some idea how long the frontal conditions will last and when you can expect the usual frontal wind shift to occur.

Satellite pictures can be more valuable when you have two successive pictures

Satellite pictures may show you when the break in the weather will come.

taken perhaps a few hours apart. From these you will be able to see the speed of travel of the weather features, and by using these in conjunction with any weather maps you should have a better handle on the weather. Sophisticated software can take successive satellite pictures and transform them into a moving picture of the weather, like those you see on TV. These give a better picture of what is going on – but remember that you are watching history.

Weather charts

Weather charts come in many different formats. There are basic weather charts in black and white showing isobars and weather fronts, which are usually issued every 12 hours.

You need a considerable understanding of meteorology to get the wind information from these, but they can serve to show how the low- and high-pressure areas and associated weather fronts are moving, which will help you build up that mental picture of the weather and its expected changes. The next step is to have this type of isobar chart animated, so that instead of one static chart for every 12 hours or so, you have a rolling picture, giving a much better idea of the movement of the various influences.

Then there are charts that focus on specific aspects of the weather – air and sea temperature, rain, wind etc. These can be found in rolling as well as static form and tend to be computer-generated from the basic weather information. The wind charts are probably of most use and show how the wind will change direction over the next few days and how it will vary in strength. Some of these charts use arrows for wind direction, with feathers on the tails to indicate strength, while others use a different colour for different wind strengths and these, combined with the arrows, can make it easier to see the big picture. The information available now also extends to charts of expected wave heights, but these do not take account of the influences of the land, tides and currents so need to be taken with a pinch of salt within 30 miles of land, or sometimes more – and when sailing it is the wind you are primarily interested in anyway.

Wind and waves

Weather information is now presented in such a precise form that it is difficult to find grounds to challenge what is shown; yet the charts give no indication of the level of accuracy or confidence in the forecast. You do not know whether the forecaster or the computer has programmed in a margin of error just to be on the safe side and is showing wind strengths slightly higher than expected; on the other hand, the wind strength shown in forecasts is that of the steady wind, and you could encounter wind gusts nearly twice this strength. Predicted gusts are rarely shown on weather charts, but could be of considerable concern to sailboats.

It is the same with waves – the heights shown on wave charts tend to be the significant wave height, the average height of the third of the highest waves. That can be a useful guide – but lurking among them could be waves of twice or even, much more rarely, three times the average height. These larger than normal waves could affect your progress considerably; but fortunately they tend to occur only in more extreme weather conditions, when – unless you are an ocean traveller – you are likely to be snug in harbour.

Wind gusts

This table gives an indication of the factors by which to multiply the forecast winds to get a guide to the strength of gusts that can occur.

	Wind speed range	Factor for maximum gust speed	Factor for mean gust speed
Daytime	Force 3–4 Force 4–5 Force 5–6	2.0 1.8 1.6	1.6 1.5 1.4
Night-time	Force 3–4 Force 4–5 Force 5–6	1.9 1.8 1.7	1.5 1.4 1.4

The forecast wind strengths do not allow for gusts and, as the table shows, the wind in gusts can be up to twice the forecast wind strength. Gusts of wind are something you need to consider carefully when sailing because the increase in wind strength can be considerable in the short term. Gusts can occur with little or no warning and last for little more than a few seconds up to five minutes. When under sail you need to have a reserve in hand so in a fresh breeze you do not want to have the maximum sail area up. Another point to consider with gusts is that there is usually a change in wind direction of between 20° and 30° clockwise when a gust appears. Being aware of this can be important when running downwind, but of course you also need to cope with this when running close-hauled. They will not cause you so much concern except in slowing your progress, but just as there are gusts that increase wind strength, there are lulls where it decreases. Because of their temporary nature there is little point in increasing sail area during a lull because, like gusts, these are a short-lived phenomenon.

Interpreting the forecast

There are two factors to consider when you get the forecast. Firstly, the forecast usually covers a 24-hour period, so the forecaster is predicting the weather for 24 hours from the time of the forecast. By the time you receive the forecast it will be at least six hours old because it takes time to process and distribute the information. With this delay, many aspects of the forecast may have changed, particularly in a fast-changing weather situation. Because it covers a 24-hour period, the forecaster will tend to look at a worst-case scenario and give the possible maximum wind that will occur over the 24 hours.

These clouds show a bit of activity and there could be squalls under them.

You may wonder why these forecasts often sound quite imprecise – for example, 'wind force 4 to 5 and occasionally force 6'. Now there is a forecast that leaves you guessing! A force 4 wind on the Beaufort Scale is probably alright for you to make a passage. Force 5 may leave you wondering if it would be better to stay in harbour, but you could go if the wind is not on the nose. That 'occasional force 6' could be the decider and make you think you should definitely stay put. Those forecast wind strengths cover speeds from 11 knots at the bottom end of force 4 up to 27 knots at the top end of force 6, and the trouble is you don't know which of these strengths it will be in your area. Surely the forecasters can do better than that?

Of course they can – but you have to remember that their forecast relates to a defined area of sea, which might stretch over 300 or 400 miles. Over that distance the weather could vary considerably – it might be a fresh wind on one side of the area and even stronger on the other side, and the poor forecaster has to cover all these possibilities in one simple forecast. Hence a wide spread of wind strengths may be introduced to cover all the possibilities for the area, so don't look for high accuracy in most radio weather forecasts as far as wind strength is concerned.

Using the Beaufort Scale

The Beaufort Scale is something of an enigma and it works in two ways. If you know the wind speed, it will indicate the sort of sea conditions that might be associated with that speed. Conversely, the sea conditions being experienced will give you an idea of the wind speed. So the Beaufort Scale is really a translation table with alternative uses in port and out at sea.

In harbour, the main use of the Beaufort Scale is to give you an idea from the forecast wind speed of the sea conditions you could expect to find outside. This is very useful, and with experience you will automatically be able to translate the forecast wind speed or force into sea conditions without reference to the table.

When you are out at sea, the Beaufort Scale will enable you to make a judgement about the wind strength from the sea conditions you are experiencing. Again, with experience you will do this almost automatically, and this guide to the wind speed will enable you to judge the conditions being experienced in relation to the forecast.

Bear in mind that the sea conditions described in the Beaufort Scale are those you might expect to find out in the open ocean where the sea in not affected by tidal flows, shallow water or a restricted fetch. In inshore water many factors can affect the state of the sea, but the Beaufort Scale can still provide a good guide although it does need a bit of experience if it is to be used to maximum advantage.

Most weather forecasts still use the Beaufort Scale numbers when describing wind strength because one number covers a range of wind speeds, making the forecast simpler. This range of speeds is about the level of accuracy you can expect from the forecast of the wind strength, so it is a tidy way of prediction.

You can't see the wind but you can see its effect on the sea.

The Beaufort Scale

Beaufort Scale number	Mean wind speed in knots	Limits of wind speed in knots	Description	Sea criteria
0	00	Less than 1	Calm	Sea like a mirror
1	02	1–3	Light air	Ripples with the appearance of scales but without foam crests
2	05	4–6	Light breeze	Small wavelets, still short but more pronounced. Crests have a glassy appearance but do not break.
3	09	7–10	Gentle breeze	Large Wavelets. Crests begin to break. Foam of glassy appearance. Perhaps scattered white horses.
4	13	11–16	Moderate breeze	Small waves, becoming longer. Fairly frequent white horses.
5	19	17–21	Fresh breeze	Moderate waves taking a more pronounced long form. Many white horses are formed.
6	24	22–27	Strong breeze	Large waves begin to form. White foam crests are more extensive everywhere and probably some spray
7	30	28–33	Near gale	Sea heaps up and white foam from breaking waves begins to be blown in streaks along the direction of the wind.
8	37	34–40	Gale	Moderately high waves of greater length. Edges of crests begin to break into spindrift. The foam is blown in well-marked streaks along the direction of the wind.
9	44	41–47	Strong gale	High waves and dense streaks of foam along the direction of the wind. Crests of waves begin to topple, tumble and roll over. Spray may affect visibility.
10	52	48–55	Storm	Very high waves with long overhanging crests. The resulting foam is blown in dense white streaks along the direction of the wind. The surface of the sea takes a white appearance and the tumbling of the sea becomes heavy and shock-like. Visibility affected.
11	60	56–63	Violent storm	Exceptionally high waves. The sea is covered with long white patches of foam lying along the direction of the wind. The edges of the wave crests are blown into froth and visibility is affected.
12	–	64 and over	Hurricane	The air is filled with foam and spray. The sea is completely white with driving spray. Visibility very seriously affected.

How it all works

This is where you come into the equation. If you have access to a weather chart showing the isobars, with a bit of experience you will be able to visualise how the weather is developing. Remember the weather is very rarely static but a volatile thing with areas of low and high pressure moving all the time, in relation both to each other and to the land. The general direction of weather travel in the Northern hemisphere is from west to east. Then there are the associated weather fronts, both cold and warm, and occlusions associated mainly with areas of low pressure, and these also move in sequence with their associated low-pressure areas and can bring changes in both wind direction and speed. So if you compare a couple of sequential weather charts, perhaps 12 hours apart, you can see how the weather is moving in terms of direction and speed. Usually, the deeper a depression, the faster it moves, and the table shows this variation.

Large depression	Can be stationary or move quite slowly unless very deep, when it will move faster
Small intense depression	Can move at speeds up to 60 knots
Normal depression	20–40 knots
Warm front	Will usually move slightly faster than its associated depression
Cold front	Will normally move slightly faster than the warm front

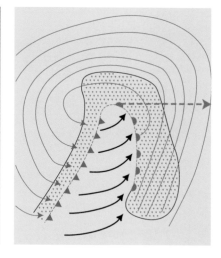

The rain areas, isobars and fronts of a typical low pressure area.

The following tables show how the weather changes as a front passes through. It is these factors that give you a clue about weather changes and how they will affect you. You can relate what you see out of the window to what the weather is doing or going to do in many cases.

The passage of a warm front is usually a slow process, with the wind direction changing slowly; but with a cold front you can encounter dramatic changes. When the squalls associated with a cold front have stopped you can find the wind changing direction by 70° or 80° in a short space of time. If you know that a cold front is going to pass through the area, you may be able to take advantage of this if, for example, you round a headland with the wind on the nose and then the wind swings round, giving you a fair wind to the next headland.

It would be ideal if you could plan passages with this degree of certainty but with the weather nothing is cast in stone as far as timing is concerned, and while you need to be able to predict change and be on the lookout for it, when the change actually happens it is not likely to be at your convenience. Racing sailors have to be past masters at knowing about wind shifts and when they will occur, but when cruising you tend to focus on the bigger weather picture and while you may know that a change is coming, you may not be certain of its timing.

Cold front

Element	In advance of the front	At the front	After the front has passed
Pressure	Falls	Sudden rise	Slow continuous rise
Wind	Backs and increases	Veers suddenly, often with line squalls and severe winds	Slowly backing after squalls then steady
Temperature	Steady but sometimes a slight fall in rain	Sudden fall	Little change
Cloud	Altocumulus and Altostratus followed by cumulonimbus	Cumulonimbus with fractostratus or low nimbostratus	Lifts rapidly but cumulus or cumulonimbus may develop
Weather	Some rain with possible thunder	Heavy rain, possibly with hail and thunder	Heavy rain then fine periods and showers
Visibility	Poor with some fog	Temporary deterioration then rapid improvement	Very good

Warm front

Element	In advance of the front	At the front	After the front has passed
Pressure	Steady fall	Fall ceases	Little change
Wind	Backs and increases	Veers and decreases	Steady
Temperature	Steady or slow rise	Rises slowly	Little change
Cloud	Cirrus, cirrostratus, altostratus, nimbostratus in succession	Low nimbostratus and fractostratus	Stratus and stratocumulus
Weather	Continuous rain or snow	Precipitation almost stops	Fair or intermittent slight rain or drizzle
Visibility	Good except in the rain or snow	Poor with mist and low cloud reducing visibility	Often poor with low cloud and mist or fog

Timing of the charts

There is a lot of activity in this approaching frontal system.

New weather charts are drawn up every 12 hours, although this may change to every six hours as the forecasters use more powerful computers to speed things up. These charts are the basis from which the forecaster produces his forecasts, converting the isobar lines into wind strengths and direction. The closer together the isobars, the higher the wind strength, and some charts enable you to measure the distance between the isobars and compare them on a scale, so you can forecast the wind strength yourself. The wind will normally blow along the line of the isobars or close to that direction, usually angled inwards towards the lower pressure area. If you study the charts, you may see that the isobars are closer together on one side of the forecast sea area than on the other, meaning the wind strengths will vary in different parts of the same forecast area.

Those wind strengths are only valid at the time of that particular chart. Twelve hours later, when the next chart is produced, the wind strengths could have varied over the forecast area because the weather is moving across the area. This is where you can pick up clues about the timing of different wind strengths and when you might encounter that force 4 of the forecast rather than the force 6 part. It requires some experience to make this sort of judgement, and the best thing when making a weather assessment before setting out on a leg of your cruise is to look at the weather charts for several days before you set off and build up a picture of how the weather patterns are developing and changing. In a sea area like the English Channel, there may be a gale blowing in the western section with a gale forecast for the eastern section as well, because that strong

Keeping up to date

These days most skippers take a laptop computer with them when they are cruising and Wi-Fi connections are available in most marinas, so there should be no problem accessing the required weather charts. You may not have Internet availability when you are out at sea, but the charts obtained in harbour will last out for the time you are at sea if you are just on day passages. If you plan to anchor, or even pick up a mooring, it could prove more difficult, but dongles that fit into a USB port can give you Internet access for a fee. Another option is a suitable App for an iPhone, but most of this weather information is land based rather than marine. I have a phone App that gives weather forecasts for every three hours ahead for the next five days for harbours around the country, but I use this more a guide than a precise forecast.

Weather charts obtained from the Internet in harbour will last out for the time you are at sea if you are just on day or overnight passages. At sea you can get updates from the forecasts that come over the radio, either the VHF marine radio or the normal broadcast channels, so hopefully you can keep up to date with changes. These radio forecasts make a good starting point to listening at sea and if you become familiar with one radio forecast source you will learn how to fine-tune this to get the results you want.

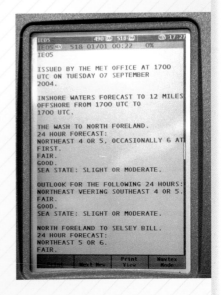

Navtex weather information obtained through the Internet.

wind will spread up the Channel as the low pressure moves through within the 24 hours of the forecast. You may be able to complete a passage before that storm comes through if you are in the eastern section of the Channel, or get out after the strong winds have died away if you are in the west. This can be a high-risk strategy and you need to tread carefully but this shows that you can negotiate with the weather.

When studying the forecast, you are only really interested in what the weather will be doing along the route you propose to take. I was returning from a cruise along the English Channel and was frustrated because strong winds had forced us to take shelter in harbour when we were just 30 miles from the home port. The forecast looked pretty grim for a couple of days ahead, so I took professional advice from a weather forecaster. After studying the charts, he said that if we left at 1500 we would find a gap in the strong winds that would give us the three hours we needed to get home. It sounded too good to be true but it was worth a try, and we could always turn back or divert if conditions deteriorated. Sure enough, he was absolutely right and we found our gap of moderate conditions and made it back to the home port with the wind just starting to increase again as we entered harbour.

That level of accurate prediction is possible with detailed forecasting but cannot be covered by the much more general type of forecast normally available on the radio or even on the Internet. Most professional forecasters these days operate as a business because an accurate forecast for a specific area is worth money so they are not going to give away such high level accuracy for nothing. We had to pay quite a lot for that accurate forecast but in those circumstances it was worth every penny.

Creating your own forecast

Basic forecast information, such as the weather charts found on the Internet, is generally quite accurate but you may not be sure of their provenance or how frequently they are updated. Twelve-hour updates are the norm when the computers are run but it could be another six hours before the actual forecast becomes available. From this basic information you can make your own interpretation of the weather, assessing how it is moving and at what speed. You want to know what it is going to be like where you plan to go and it is possible to work out the timing and magnitude of changes, perhaps not with the same accuracy as a professional but accurately enough to allow you perhaps to make a passage even when the forecasts suggest that it is not prudent. It can be a tough call sometimes and you need to err on the side of safety; but there can be enormous satisfaction in getting it right.

I had to do this when we were attempting Atlantic records a few years ago and I was the weather planner. Trying to forecast the wind and sea conditions over 3,000 miles of ocean for over three days ahead was quite a challenge, but first of all you narrow it down to what the weather will be like at the particular times along the route where you hope to be at a particular time. It doesn't matter if there is a strong wind ahead of you as long as it will die away by the time you reach that location. A storm coming up behind you calls for careful judgement as to the speed of the storm and whether you can outrun it; but with our 40 knots plus speed we could outrun most of the weather patterns of a summer in the Atlantic. When you are in mid Atlantic and have nowhere to run for shelter, it does focus the mind on making the right judgement and you do add in safety margins; but always you have to bear in mind that forecasts are just that, a forecast or a best judgement about what the weather will be. Forecasters offer no guarantees about the detailed accuracy of a forecast but you can be reasonably comfortable that it will be at least 80 per cent accurate and probably much higher – the only problem is that you don't know which 80 per cent is correct. It is when the weather is in a fast-changing pattern that short-term changes for the worse may occur, but as those patterns occur mainly in wild and stormy conditions you are not likely to be out there or even considering going to sea during those periods.

Local winds

As much of your cruising under sail will be along the coast, you will need to be aware of the various types of local wind you might encounter. Local winds are mainly caused by the difference in temperature between the sea and the land or by the topography of the land, or a combination of both, and you can often take advantage of them to make better progress. In general, local winds will not be very strong except when the general wind patterns are strong. You need to be particularly aware of these local winds when you are sailing along a coastline with the wind off the land. This can often give great sailing conditions, with a good breeze but slight or moderate sea conditions. You might sail in a force 6 when the wind was off the land for the whole voyage, but under these conditions you could also experience some quite violent winds.

This can be very much the case when there is a river valley opening up along a coast that is mainly high cliffs. The cliffs will offer good shelter from the wind, although you may not want to sail too close inshore because you can then be exposed to the often erratic winds and squalls generated as the wind over the land suddenly finds the void space at the edge of the cliff. You will find the wind is concentrated at the point where the cliffs give way to a

'...A storm coming up behind you calls for careful judgement.'

Right: You can find fresh winds funnelled through narrow channels.

Sea breezes

Sea breezes are a well-known phenomenon that are sometimes mentioned in the forecast and can turn the predicted wind on its head. Sea breezes are not likely to have a significant effect on sea conditions because they are generally light or moderate and there is very limited fetch.

To understand sea breezes, you first need to know how they come about. The primary cause is the land heating up in the daytime. Land invariably heats up more quickly than the sea, causing the wind over the land to rise as it is heated. To fill the void that this creates, cooler air from over the sea is sucked in at low level. This air is the sea breeze; the warm air over the land then cools as it rises and in so doing tends to flow out to sea and drop, so that eventually a circular airflow is created. This circuit of warming and cooling is a small self-contained weather system and usually

starts up after midday when the land has warmed up considerably.

There are two things to note about sea breezes. The first is that they are only likely to be felt up to a few miles offshore, probably no more than 5 miles. Secondly, their effect on the prevailing wind will depend on its direction. If it is coming in off the sea and blowing towards the shore, then it will be strengthened by the sea breeze. Conversely, if the prevailing wind is off the land then the two winds could possibly cancel each other out or there could be a reversal of wind direction. Much will depend on the relative strengths of the two winds.

The situation becomes more complex when the wind is flowing along the coast. Again, the relative strengths of the two winds will determine the wind direction that will prevail. In calm

conditions a sea breeze is likely to be around force 3 or 4, so a wind along the coast at the same strength would produce a resultant wind at an angle of about 45 degrees to the coastline. Stronger winds will increase this angle and lesser winds will reduce it, but it is very hard to calculate just what the final effect is likely to be.

Sea breezes die out an hour or two before sunset and if the land cools quickly then the reverse effect could occur, with a wind flowing from the land to the sea. You are only likely to encounter sea breezes of any significance in the summer when the sun is hot enough to heat the land to a temperature considerably higher than the sea. The presence of a sea breeze can often be detected as a line of cloud over the coastline, indicating where the rising air over the land is being cooled as it rises.

low valley, and the strength can rise by a couple of numbers on the Beaufort Scale as the wind pours down the valley and out to sea. You find the same in reverse when the wind is blowing in from seaward – it strengthens as it focuses on that river valley area as the easy route to pour inland. Most valley winds are quite local but the mistral, found in the Mediterranean, is essentially a valley wind blowing down the Rhône Valley and it can affect a considerable area of the sea offshore. This is a cold wind where the air is denser and thus seeks to roll down the valley, accelerating as it does so.

It is easy to assume that you will get a good lee from the land and that conditions will be good when tucked up below it. However, don't be fooled – if the land comes down in a steep slope to the shore, that slope can provide a path for the wind to accelerate, often in the form of vicious squalls. I have found these squalls when sailing off the west coast of Scotland, where the mountains create a significant turbulence and one squall was serious enough to spin us right round through 360°. You can encounter similar squalls along much of the mountainous Mediterranean coastline and when the wind is fresh you often see these squalls coming across the water as an area of whipped-up spray, perhaps no more than 100 metres (110 yards) across.

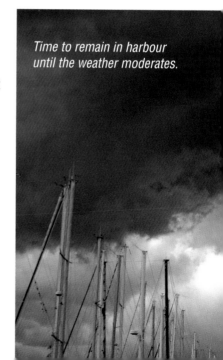

Time to remain in harbour until the weather moderates.

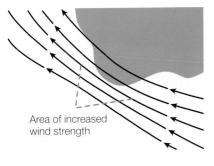

Area of increased
wind strength

Wind sweeping past a headland tends to contour round the end of the headland even when the land is low lying. This tends to compress the air flow, giving stronger winds around the headland.

When the wind is blowing more or less along the line of the coast, expect to find a stronger wind around headlands where the airflow gets compressed.

This can be quite a feature around high prominent headlands and these are also the areas where you might find tide rips, so both the wind and sea conditions can be more severe. Keeping well offshore should take you into more moderate conditions but might entail a considerable diversion. Headlands are always a significant point in any passage, because not only can you find changing and often more severe conditions around the headland but they usually mean an alteration of course and picking up a new wind on the far side, so extra vigilance is needed here.

Islands can present a particular problem with local winds. Not only will you get winds from different directions at various points around the island but you can also encounter squalls on the lee side, as well as various components of the winds where they find a way to travel both around and over the island and meet up again. Then there is the passage between an island and the mainland where the wind can be funnelled through and gain in strength. It is usual to find not only an increase in the wind strength in narrow passages but also that the wind will tend to follow the line of the channel even though the main airflow might be different. In these channels you will have either a head wind or a following wind despite the direction of the prevailing wind and this can be found particularly among the islands off Scotland and along the coasts of Norway.

Thunderstorms

Thunderstorms can present quite a threat to a sailboat because of the often intense winds they can generate. You are likely to encounter one of two main types of thunderstorm at sea – the frontal thunderstorm, generated from the activity in a cold front, and the heat thunderstorm, which is usually generated over land as the air is heated but can then move out to sea.

We tend to think of thunderstorms as just bringing heavy rain and reduced visibility for a while, perhaps associated with some spectacular lightning displays. However, do not underestimate thunderstorms as they can represent one of the more violent forms of local weather. They can produce some quite savage local winds and while these are not likely to last long enough to generate any serious change in the sea conditions, the heavy rain found in thunderstorms can be a short-term problem for sailboats and indeed boats of all types.

The sort of thunderstorms that form out at sea are usually associated with an active cold front. This can be particularly the case when the temperature difference between the warm and colder air masses in the front is considerable, as is often found in a very active frontal system. Such an active front can sometimes be recognised by the considerable wind shift that occurs, and this alone can be enough to start the process of a thunderstorm forming. Combine this wind shift with the temperature differences associated with the front and you have the recipe for the very active conditions that lead to thunderstorms.

For a heat thunderstorm, it is the hot air rising over heated land on a hot summer day that starts the circulation going. The heated air rises and then cools, which starts the vertical circulation of air often found in a thunderstorm. When the air rises far enough, it meets up with the fast-moving winds of the upper atmosphere and this leads to the formation of the distinctive 'anvil' cloud of a fully formed thunderstorm. Once started, the quite violent

air circulation of a thunderstorm can continue for quite a while and the thunderstorm will move, usually in the direction of the upper wind – the anvil cloud can give a clue to its direction of movement. The interaction between the various moving air masses in a thunderstorm generates the static electricity that produces the thunder and lightning, and also creates the heavy rain by mixing the hot and colder air masses, when the moisture can condense out. Thunderstorms created over the land can move out over the sea and cause problems for small craft.

In daylight you should be able to recognize a thunderstorm from quite a distance, and they are best avoided. You can do this in a sailboat by heading to one side or the other of the storm, but it is obviously better to head towards the lee side away from the direction of travel. It is certainly advisable to shorten sail and probably even better to drop the sails altogether and proceed under motor so that you reduce the risk when being struck by the sudden very fierce winds of the storm. Thunderstorms can be easily recognized by the anvil cloud when they are fully formed, but the very dark base cloud can be another indicator. At night it is the lightning that reveals their presence, but this can be visible over quite a large area of the sky in a frontal system and it is not always easy to pinpoint just where the storm is located. Thunderstorms can occur at any time of the year when they are associated with cold fronts but you are more likely to encounter them in the summer when local variations in temperatures can trigger the process.

Obviously thunderstorms are best avoided if the navigation situation allows you the freedom to vary your course. The avoidance tactics are similar in many ways to those you might use in collision avoidance situations with other craft – except that it would be sensible always to allow the thunderstorm the right of way.

You can usually pick out a thunderstorm very clearly on radar if you have one, and this makes avoidance much easier. The heavy rain found in the thunderstorm creates a large and usually quite sharp-edged target that can be quite irregular in shape and will be considerably larger than any ship target, so it is unlikely that it can be mistaken for anything else. It can look something like the radar return from an island, but your navigation situation should soon tell you whether there is an island in the position shown on the radar. The only situation where it might not be easy to see a thunderstorm on the radar would be when it is over or close to the land, when the thunderstorm image could merge with the land returns.

Left: A thunderstorm developing on the horizon.

Right: Waterspouts are definitely best avoided.

A thunderstorm can show up on the radar at up to 20 miles but if you are operating on the 12-mile range used for normal navigation, then detection at this distance should still allow plenty of time for avoidance manoeuvres. If you put the bearing cursor of the radar on the centre of the thunderstorm target, you know you will be passing clear if the thunderstorm return moves away from the bearing cursor. There ought to be a significant movement of the target in relation to the bearing cursor if you plan to pass well clear.

If the bearing of the thunderstorm target remains steady or only changes slightly in relation to the bearing cursor over a period of a few minutes, it could be time to alter course if you want to clear the thunderstorm. You will need to make a significant alteration of course of, say, 30° or more to have a significant effect on the relative movement of the thunderstorm and your boat. At night, radar detection of a thunderstorm can be a great help in avoidance tactics.

Squalls

Squalls are different from gusts in that they are more predicable, at least in the short term, and you are likely to get some warning of their arrival in daylight, although night-time detection can present problems. Squalls will be found where two airflows mix or where there is a rising airflow due to warming or similar disturbances. You will almost certainly find squalls along a cold front due to the intensity of the front and the mixing of the air masses. Squalls are less likely along a warm front where the mixing of the airflows is less intense; and there is very little chance of finding squalls in an occluded front, where conditions tend to be much less active.

Squalls of a milder form can be found under areas of cloud where the cloud indicates a mixing of air as warmer air rises. Here the wind increase in the squall is likely to be moderate owing to the less intense nature of the activity, but even such a temporary increase can be useful for sailboats if you can detect it on a day of light winds. This type of squall will be found mostly in the summer when the local heating can be more intense.

Squalls can often be found near land when the wind is stronger, particularly if the wind is off the land or along the coastline and the land is fairly high. In this situation it is the land that interferes with the flow of air and creates eddies in the flow that can develop into squalls.

A squall can last up to an hour but is more likely to be of shorter duration and no more than 15 minutes. The cloud activity is likely to be your early warning sign of an approaching squall – expect to experience quite sharp squalls when you see intense cloud activity. In many ways, squalls are a milder form of thunderstorm activity and will often be accompanied by rain, which will help you to identify their presence from a distance. You can even track the progress of a squall if it is associated with rain, which can be useful if you feel the need to take avoiding action.

At night the detection of squalls can be difficult. There will be little in the way of visual indication until the squall hits you, although if there is associated rain it should be possible to pick it up on radar. The increased wind found in a squall may call for a shortening of sail for the duration, and also be aware that there can be a temporary change in wind direction as the squall passes through.

An approaching squall with heavy rain and active winds.

A line squall is a very distinctive feature and can hide violent winds.

Anticipating sea conditions

By now you have a good idea of what the wind will be like during your proposed passage – but that is only half the story. Now you need to translate this wind strength and direction into what the sea conditions will be like, because it is those waves, not the wind, that will dictate your safety and your progress. A well-found cruising yacht will cope with a wide range of sea conditions but as you will normally be cruising for enjoyment, the discomfort of rougher seas might dictate caution. Conditions where you consider taking in a reef will suggest you are entering the discomfort zone as far as cruising sailing is concerned.

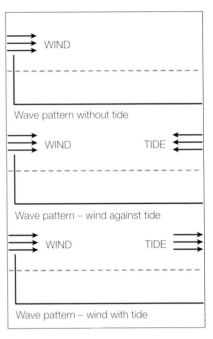

The way in which the wave profile is modified under the influence of the currents or tide.

Wind against tide can produce some nasty sea conditions.

Forecasts rarely include wave heights for coastal waters but the Beaufort Scale gives you some idea of the size of waves to expect in various wind strengths. In addition, you need to look out for sea areas where you might encounter more extreme wave conditions – these could be in tidal races, around headlands and in shoal areas. Many of the more severe areas will be marked on the chart but be aware of finding very uncomfortable short steep seas when the wind is blowing against a strong tide. Areas like the Portland Race can generate vicious sea conditions, which, at certain states of the wind and tide, can be dangerous to small craft. Similar but less severe conditions can be found around many prominent headlands and you can also find these conditions in narrow channels where the tidal flow and the wind are compressed into a steep-sided channel, with a consequent increase in the severity of the waves. You find this effect through the Strait of Bonifacio between Corsica and Sardinia, an area noted for its wild conditions, where the wind can increase by one or two numbers on the Beaufort Scale. Another Mediterranean area noted for its increased winds is the Straits of Messina, particularly when the wind is from the south and is funnelled into a narrower and narrower passage.

This line squall sweeping in from the Atlantic will generate some lively sea conditions.

Shallow water

You can see the effect of shallow water on waves when you stand on a beach where waves are breaking. Hopefully you will never be this close up and personal with shallow water in your boat, but further out to sea a patch of relatively shallow water can cause waves to rear up in height and shorten in wavelength as they pass over the shallows, particularly if it is a deep ocean swell coming inshore. This effect is unlikely to be significant in the sort of weather conditions in which you will be cruising, but in rougher conditions the bigger waves and possibly breaking crests could be a problem even when the water is deep enough for you to make a safe passage across it. Shallow water can be a significant factor in changing the wave patterns when it lies off a headland where there may be strong tides running, and shallow harbour entrances with a bar across them can be dangerous with an ebb tide and with onshore winds.

When the waves have breaking crests like this it is probably time to seek shelter.

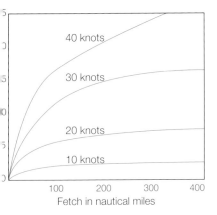

A graph showing the way that wave height increases with fetch in various wind strengths.

Tides

It is tides that can have the most significant effect on the sea conditions you find when you are cruising, and the absence of any tidal streams or currents in the Mediterranean is, I am sure, one of the reasons you tend to encounter far more consistent sea conditions there. With tides, the whole body of water on which you are sailing is moving, often at considerable speeds. If that body of water is moving against the wind, then the wavelength will shorten, which in turn means that the waves become steeper. This steeper wave gradient can make life quite uncomfortable for a cruising yacht because there is less time for the boat to recover from passing over one wave before it has to cope with the next one. Also, the steeper the wave, the more likely it is to break at the crest, and it only takes a wave gradient of around 18° before the wave starts to break, which adds to the difficulty and danger when you are sailing a boat through it.

The change in sea conditions when the wind is against the tide will vary according to the strength of the tidal stream. Out in the open sea, away from the land, the tide is unlikely to run at more than 2 knots, which, while you will notice the waves becoming steeper, is not likely to have a significant effect on your progress. However, when you get inshore the rate of the tidal stream can vary considerably, particularly where the flow of water gets squeezed around headlands, where you might find that the general flow of a 2-knot stream increases to double that figure. Along the English Channel there are many headlands where you see this effect, notably at Portland Bill, Start Point and the Lizard, where the headlands stick well out into the tidal stream and disrupt the smooth flow of the water.

The flow of the tidal streams can have a significant impact of your passage, not just by adding or subtracting a knot or two to your speed but also on the sea conditions. The change from rough to smooth as the tide changes can be quite dramatic in areas like the Bristol Channel, where the tide turns very quickly with less than half an hour of slack water, and you need to be prepared for this. The short steep seas of wind against the tide can mean trouble for a small cruiser in fresh winds, so the tidal atlas should be your bible when you plan a cruise in northern waters and working the tides is a vital part of passage planning.

Local conditions

Just as you need to bring in your own personal assessment of the wind conditions you may expect from the broad-brush statements of the weather forecast, so you need to translate the effects of local conditions on both the wind strength and the sea conditions. This becomes a lot easier without the effect of tidal streams, which is why the Mediterranean is attractive for sailing; but here the land adjacent to the sea tends to be a lot higher than in Northern Europe and there can be bigger temperature variations between land and sea, so the wind changes influenced by the land can be more significant. I have experienced some very lively conditions when the fetch was quite small, simply because the wind was whistling down a valley and creating a patch of wild water in an area where it should have been quite comfortable.

Please don't be put off by all this talk of difficult and possibly dangerous conditions. Most can be anticipated, and in the sort of conditions where you go cruising they will be less evident; but just keep the possibilities at the back of your mind so you are not taken by surprise.

5

Sailing

Harnessing the wind

The wind is a strange thing – you can feel it and you can observe its effect, but you cannot see it. When you are cruising under sail you harness this unseen power to take you to your destination. When you think about it, it is a really strange phenomenon – but man has been harnessing the wind to sail for hundreds of years, and now you have the benefit of all this experience to power you across the sea. The wind is one of the greenest forms of energy and harnessing its power on a sailboat has become a technical marvel.

The mechanics of sailing are quite complex but here we will explore at least some of the aspects of sailing and sail trim that can help your cruising. When you are cruising under sail you are not looking to squeeze the last ounce of sailing performance from the rig – the accent is more on comfortable cruising. Naturally you want the sails to work efficiently, but you are probably not going to trim them constantly to get them working at their maximum. Remember, this is a pleasure cruise you are on – although of course some sailors will get their pleasure from constant sail trimming to maximise their speed.

On an average cruising yacht in a fresh breeze it is usually possible to sail quite close to the maximum speed of the hull, which for a 35 footer would be around 7½ knots. Even if you double the power available from the sails, there will hardly be any increase in speed once this maximum has been reached. Racing yachtsmen spend a lot of time and money on trying to find the extra power from the sails to gain a slight bit of extra speed, but the improvements are very slight compared with the cost because they are operating close to their maximum hull speed anyway. Lower down the speed scale, a reduction in the available power by, say, a half from what is required to achieve the maximum will still give good performance, and a 35 foot hull should still give speeds of over 6 knots. You can see this in the performance when the vessel is motoring – a considerable reduction in rpm from that given top speed will have little effect on performance provided the boat is generously powered, and will give a good saving in fuel while the speed may drop by only 1 knot. So sailing at 6 knots would be considered quite adequate by most owners and can be achieved with a fairly simple rig and sails that are neither too large nor too heavy for two people to handle.

Hull speed is dictated by the length of the hull, although width is relevant as well – the narrower the hull, the higher the hull speed. This is why catamarans can reach higher speeds, even though they are still displacement hulls – their narrow hulls slip through the water easily. Most monohull cruising yachts are full displacement hulls and the hull speed is dictated more or less by their waterline length. A vertical bow increases the waterline length for a given overall length, which is why it is the fashion these days. Weight is also important,

Sail systems have got a lot simpler than those on this square rigger.

The simple rig on this catamaran is designed for easy handling.

Right: Cruising yachts are not normally looking for the ultimate in efficiency from their sails.

particularly in light winds – the heavy motor sailer type of yacht tends to be sluggish in light winds, while a light cruiser/racer will still keep going. The ballast in the keel, which helps to keep the yacht upright when close-hauled, does not help performance but is essential for stability – another reason multihulls perform better is that they do not have to carry ballast.

Power from the sails

Given that a cruising yacht is fitted with a reasonably efficient sailing rig, the power available from the sails will be more or less proportional to their area. However, the amount of sail you carry depends on the wind strength, and a good area of lightweight sails for light winds can always be reduced in area by reefing. It is a complex area of design and a challenge for the designer of the rig because a large number of variable factors have to be considered. The rig has to produce power not only over a range of wind strengths but also on all points of sailing.

When sailing close-hauled, much of the power produced by the wind ends up trying to push the yacht sideways and perhaps only a quarter of the available power pushes the boat forward. This lateral thrust from the wind pressure is resisted by the shape of the hull and keel, which is designed to stop them making leeway sideways through the water as far as possible. The greater the hull area, the more resistance there is to sideways movement, which is why you see yachts with deep keels or centreboards. The lateral pressure of the wind also heels the yacht over, and the ballast in the keel is there to balance this. To a certain extent the effect of the wind on transverse heeling is self-compensating, because the further the boat heels over, the less will be the effective area of the sails exposed to the wind; and when heeled over there comes a point where the boat is not sailing so efficiently and the waterline length can reduce, so the boat slows. If the boat is heeling excessively when close-hauled, it is probably time to shorten sail. This will not only take the pressure off and allow the yacht to sail more effectively but will also make life on board more comfortable. In a gusty wind there will be times when a stronger gust comes along, making the boat heel; but with a temporary increase in wind strength like this it is probably OK to live with it rather than reduce sail, and you can always luff up into the wind to ease the pressure.

When running before the wind there is very little transverse thrust on the sails and consequently very little heeling moment. However, if the wind comes on the quarter or further towards the beam, the heeling moment will increase; but obviously if there was adequate stability in the close-hauled situation, then it will be adequate for these other situations, although you should bear in mind that the inherent stability in the hull can be reduced quite considerably when operating in a following sea, because the boat may be perched on a wave crest for some considerable time as the wave passes under. This is why there is often a quite strong rolling motion to a boat when running before the wind, which can be exaggerated with the wind aft because there is not the transverse pressure on the sails to help reduce the rolling – another good reason to offset the course if the wind is right astern.

'…the amount of sail you carry depends on the wind strength.'

Setting the sails

When setting the sails you want to get balance into the boat and in a close-hauled tack the sideways pressure generated by the sails, which is focused on their centre of effort (COE), should be more or less in a vertical line about the centre of lateral resistance (CLR) of the hull. The COE of the sails is more or less their combined geometric centre seen from the side and the CLR is the geometric centre of the underwater part of the hull at any given time. When the two are in line, the steering will be more or less neutral. If the COE moves forward, then the wind will want to blow the bow downwind and you have lee helm. If it moves aft of the CLR, then you have weather helm. Small amounts of these two helm situations are not a problem but if they become more noticeable then you might want to adjust the sails to try to find a better balance. A smaller jib will compensate for lee helm or perhaps just easing the sheets a fraction, whereas with weather helm you could try easing the main to reduce its effect.

It is almost impossible to get a complete balance and indeed most cruising yachtsmen would not be very comfortable with this because it tends to take the feel out of the steering. Most skippers will prefer a boat that carries a modest degree of weather helm, i.e. if left to its own devices, it will round up into the wind, and this is what the designer aims for when determining the shape of the rig. This is a fail-safe situation to a certain extent, because when caught out in a sudden squall the boat will want to round up into the wind and ease the pressure.

Reefing

Probably one of the main areas where you need to consider the balance of the sails is when you start to put in reefs when the wind is freshening. Certainly in a fresh wind you will be much more conscious of the sail balance and if you simply reef the main then you are moving the COE of the sails forward, which can make the steering very heavy and difficult and possibly change the weather helm into a lee helm. This emphasises the need to keep the balance of the sails even when reefed down in strong winds by reefing both the main and the jib(s).

Well reefed down in a strong breeze.

Left: Entering harbour in a force 6 with the sails reefed down.

Above: There is plenty of power in this scrap of sail in a strong breeze.

Reefing these days is a relatively simple operation. On a cruising yacht, furling jibs are now used almost universally, with power used on larger yachts to handle the task. This makes the deployment, reefing and stowing of the jib simply a matter of pulling on the correct ropes, although you will also need to control the sheets when doing this.

The whole operation can be done from the cockpit. For the main you might have boom roller reefing, mast roller reefing or just the old-fashioned sail with reefing points that you tie in by hand. With in-mast reefing you cannot have sail battens to help shape the sail; and battens on a serious blue water cruiser sail tend to be looked on as a cause of chafe rather than a major benefit. You certainly need to keep an eye out for possible chafe on any sail with battens.

With a new crew on board it can be a good idea to go through the process of reefing so that if you have to do this at sea they will have some idea of what to do. If you find yourself in a freshening wind and you start to think about taking in a reef, then this is the time to do it. The longer you wait and the stronger the wind, the harder it will be. If the forecast suggests strong winds, setting up the reef before you leave harbour can make the job a lot simpler.

' …With a new crew on board it can be a good idea to go through the process of reefing.'

A sail that rolls up into the mast cannot use battens.

Traditional roller reefing gear with exposed gears.

Winching in the jib sheets.

Main and jib

Nearly all cruising yachts these days have a simple rig of just main and jib. The jib is usually a good size, even a genoa, which can be adjusted in size to suit the conditions from light airs to fresh breeze simply by letting the furling gear in or out.

With this type of system, all the sails can be controlled from the cockpit, which is a good safety feature and can be done when there is just one person on watch. The need to handle heavy canvas at sea has virtually disappeared and modern sailing rigs are so efficient and easy to operate. The only heavy work is hauling up the main, and even that can be mechanised if you have mast furling – and there are often mast winches to help on larger yachts.

Hydraulically powered roller reefing on the jib on a larger yacht.

Cutter and ketch rigs

There are cruising yachts with alternative rigs, such as the cutter and the ketch, where the sail area is divided up into smaller units.

The cutter, with its two headsails, gives more flexibility about the sail area that you carry and the same can be said about the ketch rig, although that was mainly developed to improve manoeuvring in the days before engines.

With a sail at each end of the yacht you can generate quite a steering effect by adjusting the sails. The bowsprit sometimes fitted to yachts with a cutter rig has almost disappeared and that extra length to take the sail anchorage points further forward can be an expensive luxury when you come to pay marina fees by the metre. For uncomplicated cruising, the simple sloop with sail-handling systems is the answer. Even lowering the main can be made much simpler by the use of 'lazy jacks', light ropes rigged on each side of the main that help to contain the sail as it is lowered so you don't immediately need sail ties to contain the canvas.

The cutter rig allows you more flexibility in the sail area to match the conditions.

The ketch rig splits up the sail area into smaller units and allows you to adjust the sail balance.

Adjusting the trim

Trimming sails to get the maximum pull is a fine art and for the purist there are many adjustments that can be made to change the shape and amount of curve in the sail and the angles to the wind. These adjustments are well covered in dedicated books on sailing but in broad terms you want to get the sails setting well and efficiently. For the foresails, the primary adjustment is the sheet and this is adjusted both by its tension, which pulls the sail in, and by the position of the car that carried the sheet lead pulley from the sail to the winch. It is pretty obvious when the sail is pulling well and you will probably only want to adjust the position of the car when the wind is abaft the beam if creases start to form in the sail.

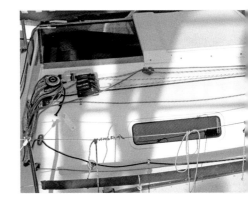

Coloured ropes help you to identify the rope you want.

Telltales – little strands of twine or threads attached to the sail – are a great guide to the effectiveness of the sail setting when close-hauled and these should be strung out horizontally to show that the wind is flowing cleanly across the sail. If you get erratic movement of the telltales on the lee side, you should let out the sheet a shade; and if they droop on the weather side, you haul in the sheet to optimise the sail. You may have them on the main as well, where the same clean airflow can be indicated. On the main there is the sheet setting and you can also make further adjustment by moving the position of the sheet anchorage point across on the sheet track, if one is fitted.

Below: A Genoa reaches well aft to give a lot of sail power in moderate winds.

Right: Rope stoppers allow one winch to be used for several ropes.

Spinnakers

Spinnakers can be a great boon in light winds when you are running before the wind and if you stick to a smaller cruising chute they should not be a problem to handle, even with a small crew. It is during setting and recovery that most people get into trouble and this is best done in the lee of the main or foresail.

There are a number of proprietary spinnaker-setting systems designed to give more control and to simplify things, and they can help by allowing you to hoist the spinnaker before it is opened out to the wind. These can be useful with a small crew because deploying and recovering the spinnaker can mean handling the spinnaker pole as well as the sail and its sheets.

You can simplify things and use the spinnaker without a pole, as is often the case with a designated cruising chute; but the pole helps a lot to get the sail out to windward so that it is not blanketed by the main and to allow it to be used over a greater range of wind angles. The spinnaker sheets need to be led well aft, where the sail can be controlled from the cockpit, and usually a pull on the windward sheet will be enough to stabilise the sail if it starts to collapse. As long as you do not get too ambitious with the spinnaker, it can improve the speed of the yacht considerably in light winds; but you want to be sure that you have a useful distance to travel on the current heading before using it, and think carefully about using one if the wind is gusty. An alternative to using a spinnaker in following winds can be poling out the foresail on the opposite side to the main to pick up the maximum amount of wind.

'…Spinnakers can be a great boon in light winds.'

Right: Great sailing with a spinnaker but you might hesitate to use one at night.

Storm sails

It used to be the fashion to carry
storm sails – heavy-duty canvas that
could stand up to storm force winds.
These sails may still be found on blue
water cruisers, but sail material has
improved so much these days that for
most cruising the standard sails will be
adequate to cope with nearly all wind
conditions. Storm sails would normally
be a loose fitted small main, often called
a try sail, and a small jib.

*Below: Yachts sailing out of the lively
seas of a tide race.*

Above: The yacht Satori *with just a scrap of sail up in the violent winds
associated with the Perfect Storm.*

Winches

The sheet winches are a vital part of the equipment these days, particularly when larger jibs or genoas are fitted. It is essential to get a good lead from the sheet block to the winch so that you do not get riding turns and the sheet should always lead up from the lead block to the winch. If you are unfortunate enough to get a riding turn where the rope turns on the winch are trapped under the incoming rope and you can't free them, it may be possible to clear this by pulling upwards on the tail end of the rope, but an alternative is to take the tail to the opposite winch and pull it out from there. With a riding turn the sheet is effectively locked so you want to clear this as soon as possible. Winch handles are always a source of frustration and the crew must be disciplined to remove them after use and return them to their dedicated stowage; and always carry spare handles on board, because they have a nasty habit of finding their way overboard.

Backstays

In general, the rigging will look after itself at sea with the backstay being the only piece that might need adjustment. There was a time when you had a backstay on each side and you needed to let one off and tighten the other on each change of tack. Now a single centreline backstay usually does the job because the mainsail and boom are sized to fit inside it and the tension is adjustable either by a screw wheel or by hydraulics. You will tend to tighten the backstay when running to compensate for the pull of the sails, but this adjustment is usually one left to the racing fraternity, who use it to introduce mast bend to improve the sail setting. Boom vangs or kickers are another adjustment to the boom setting and these, together with luff lines and other features, are all part of the racing repertoire to get the boat sailing to its maximum.

It is your choice whether you want to go into this level of sailing when you are cruising – but for most cruisers, getting a good set of sails and then sitting back and enjoying the trip is the primary aim in life.

☑ Top Tip

Points to remember

When you have a genoa or foresail that can reach as far aft as the standing rigging at the mast, you need to take care that the sail cannot chafe against the rigging or the spreaders when the sail is sheeted in tightly. The bottle screws on the lower end of the rigging are often the main source of chafe, which is why you will often see these wrapped in tape to stop sharp edges attacking the sail. Also bear in mind that when you have the full area of the sail set, it can often obstruct the view from the helm.

Taped up rigging screws to reduce the chance of chafe.

6

Entering harbour

Entering the unknown

When you leave harbour you move from the tight confines of crowded waters into the expanding horizons of the open sea. By contrast, entering harbour can be a whole new experience, because not only may the waters and the surroundings be new to you but you are entering an area where the land is closing in and where close encounters are the norm. It can be an exciting time but also one of increased tensions – you are entering the unknown, and uncertainty levels can be quite high. I love the experience, the thrill of discovery as a new harbour opens up, the excitement and the challenge; but to make it work you need to plan ahead. When you are cruising, planning ahead is the key to making most things happen in a reasonably ordered and controlled way and this applies very much when you are entering a new and unknown harbour.

However, first you have to make your landfall and find the harbour entrance. With GPS working this should be fairly straightforward, but harbour entrances are not always easy to pick out, particularly if the sun is rising or setting behind the land. A great help here can be conspicuous marks that identify the entrance, so look on the chart for anything that will help. An advantage of paper charts is that many conspicuous features are marked, whereas you rarely find them on the electronic chart.

Above: A lighthouse on each pier head at the entrance to Dover Harbour.

Left: A conspicuous lighthouse at the entrance to Palma Harbour in Majorca.

Conspicuous marks

When you cruise along a coastline, many features stand out and can be clearly identified. In the days when you used a hand-bearing compass to fix your position, these conspicuous marks were invaluable because they provided the key to knowing where you were. Today, fixing your position with bearings is rarely carried out, but the conspicuous marks along the coast can still be valuable for visual navigation because they provide strong clues about your location.

There are three main ways to use conspicuous marks. The first is simply a check on the position, and even when using GPS it is reassuring to check progress by using features on the land. If you note when the conspicuous mark is abeam and you know your course, you have a fairly accurate position line extending at right angles from your course line to the conspicuous mark.

'Conspic'

A conspicuous mark is only really valuable when it is also marked on the chart. They may be identified with annotations such as 'Spire conspic' or 'Tall building conspic'. That was fine when the survey from which the chart was generated was up to date, but today many of these so-called conspicuous objects can be either difficult to see or confusing. A church spire may be hidden from view from seaward by tall buildings erected in front of it, and several tall buildings may surround what was a single tall building when the survey was carried out, presenting a confusing picture. A look on Google Earth could help identify what might be visible.

Above right: You need to know the leading marks well to find your way into a harbour channel like this.

The second way is to use the marks as a steering reference. Steering a compass course can be tedious and takes your focus away from what is going on outside the boat. If you set the course initially by compass and then try to identify a mark on the land on or near the required heading, that mark can provide a much better temporary heading reference.

Finally, you can use a similar technique to find a harbour entrance. These do not always show up well when some way off and can be confusing. A conspicuous mark located near the entrance, such as a lighthouse or a tall chimney, can give a good clue about where the entrance lies, even when many miles away.

Below: Time to put the echo sounder on when entering harbour.

Top Tip

Echo sounder

The depth of water under a boat is an important navigation tool when you are heading in towards the land. As a general rule, the closer to land you are the shallower it becomes, but don't rely on that implicitly. Your harbour entrance may have a deep-water channel that has been dredged to allow the big ships to enter and cliffs can sometimes descend directly into quite deep water. However, even with GPS leading the way it makes sense to have the echo sounder on when approaching land.

Using depth to make a landfall

One of the main criteria of navigating safely is to maintain enough depth of water under the boat to give a good margin of safety. The main time that a boat is at risk of grounding is when making a landfall, and this is where depth measurements can be a very important indicator. Even when the GPS shows the position to be safe, an adequate depth of water showing under the keel is the important confirmation you need. When navigating, an independent check is always important reassurance and this is one of the most useful roles of the sounder.

In order to use the sounder readings in a meaningful way, you need to study the chart carefully, not only at the expected landfall point but also for a distance either side of it. When the depth drops away quickly from the land you will get less warning that you are approaching land and sudden shoaling on the sounder could mean that you are virtually on top of the land. By contrast, a gradual decrease in the depth will indicate the approach to land with adequate warning.

Gradual shoaling would appear to give the best results, but because it is gradual there will be no clear point at which you can say precisely that the boat is on a definite sounding position line. When you see the shoaling you cannot assume that you are making your landfall at the precise point you were aiming for, which is why you need to study the depths on either side of the landfall point. This study may show that the depths are too irregular to give any meaningful indication, or show gradual shoaling so that a sudden shoaling could indicate that you are off course.

The value of using soundings when making a landfall will depend on each case and you have to make that judgement. It is easy to jump to conclusions and make the sounding appear to fit what you want to see. Also soundings will not necessarily be useful when making a landfall on a rocky coastline, particularly when there are off-lying rocks, because here you can find very sudden changes of depth.

The chart can show the changes in depth that can help with navigating a harbour channel.

The wide entrance to this harbour has distinctive shallow areas.

Breaking water in a harbour entrance will indicate shallows but you may not see it until you are close.

A visual image of the harbour

Twenty years ago, when you were entering a new harbour you had the information on the chart, perhaps supplemented by information in the pilot guide. You had to translate this information into some sort of visual picture of what the harbour might be like. The pilot guide might have a photo or two, but by and large you had to rely on translating the plan view of the harbour on the chart into a 3D picture of what you might see as you entered. It could be quite a challenge and I was often amazed at the reality compared with what I had imagined. Today things are very different and, while you can now get an overlay on the chart that shows all the land features, I tend to look harbours up on Google Earth. Here you can get a much better visual image and you can zoom in for close-ups and even change the viewing angle so you will have almost a complete picture of what you will see as you enter harbour.

Right: Modern electronic charts can show a very graphic picture of harbours.

Far right: Sails roughly stowed for entering harbour can restrict visibility from the helm.

Assessing harbour entrances

When making plans for a passage, you will have a destination harbour in mind. The weather conditions may look set fair for the passage, but will they be OK for entering your chosen harbour? While many or perhaps most harbours do not have much in the way of weather restrictions for entry, give some thought to what the conditions might be like in the harbour entrance and consider whether you will be able to use the chosen harbour on arrival.

In the context of making an easy passage, you may well want to take the easy option of running downwind. When the wind is behind you, it will be blowing straight into your destination harbour. Many harbours can be entered safely in a fresh onshore wind, but consider what the conditions will be like if your chosen harbour has a shallow bar across the entrance, as is often the case when entering a river harbour – here, you could be faced with breaking seas.

An aerial view of a harbour in rough sea can show the conditions but it can be hard to assess them from sea level.

All looks well to make the entrance to this harbour.

In any harbour entrance the sea conditions are likely to be worse if there is a strong ebb tide running out of the harbour. The sea conditions can deteriorate quite dramatically even when there is not a bar and you might also experience difficult conditions when the entrance is guarded by a breakwater, which can cause a confusion of reflected waves off the vertical stone walls. Be aware that you could find quite severe local conditions when the wind is blowing into the harbour – just what you don't need at the end of a day's sailing.

In your passage planning, look also at the possibility of alternative harbours. You might encounter fog or have some other reason to shorten the passage, so in your preparation it pays to look at the various alternatives, just in case. Also check whether any of these harbours might have tidal restrictions that could limit entry times.

The challenge of the harbour entrance

Google Earth images go a long way towards building up that visual image of what you are going into when you enter harbour, but to a certain extent it takes away some of the interest and excitement of the challenge. It is up to you to decide just how much you want to know about the harbour you are visiting; but whatever your approach, planning for entering is essential. There are so many different types of harbour, ranging from the organised marina accessed directly from the sea, where entry can be straightforward, to the long winding river approach where you may be following a line of buoys marking the channel into an area that seems to get more and more restricted as you get closer to the berth. Many marinas in the Mediterranean are entered directly from the sea, giving you little time to adapt from the generous spaces of the open sea to the tight confines of the marina. It is a very sudden transition, and the marina breakwater prevents a view inside, so it pays to have some idea of what it might be like when you enter. The marina authorities will probably have allocated you a berth over the radio link, but you have to identify how the pontoons are marked or numbered and work out how to find your way around. I find these days that, in the interests of making as much money as possible from the available space,

A hand held GPS can be useful when entering harbour and will show a surprising amount of detail.

Below left: It can start to seem very crowded as the confines of the harbour close in.

Below right: A marina can be a crowded place coming in from seaward.

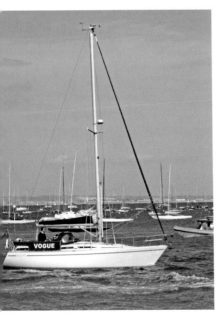

Leading marks can help you keep to the channel.

' ...Rivers with tidal entrances may need care on entry.'

Furling the jib as you come into harbour.

marinas offer less and less space to manoeuvre in, so it helps to have some sort of plan before you enter. In good conditions there should not be a problem because you will have time to stop and work things out, but if there is a fresh breeze blowing you about, you may not have the same luxury. Once again planning can help, and stopping outside to lower the sails and get the mooring ropes and fenders out will be time well spent.

Then there are the marinas in rivers and inside harbours, where there may also be a tide or current running through the marina to cope with. This can make manoeuvring tricky and you need to have a plan to get into your allocated berth before you arrive, rather than trying to make it up as you go along. When you are cruising in the Mediterranean you not only have the benefit of the generally fine weather, but also a wide selection of accessible marinas to cruise from and to. It can make life easy for the cruising yachtsman; but in northern waters, while you may face more challenging conditions, you will end up a better seaman because of the experience of coping with winds and tides as well as crowded marinas. It is all part of the cruising experience, and if you know your boat well there should be no major problems provided you plan ahead. This can be particularly important when the harbour has a river or a tidal entrance, or perhaps is also an important commercial port.

Rivers with tidal entrances may need care on entry when there is a bar or a stretch of shallow water across the entrance. In Britain you find this feature on many west-facing harbours where the seas coming in from the west meet the outgoing tide and current from the river, creating a sort of battleground at the entrance. In fresh onshore winds you should consider abandoning this harbour because of the turmoil you might find across the bar. This will be particularly severe on the ebb tide, so there is the possibility of waiting until the flood tide, when the wind and tide will be more in harmony. The problem with the breaking sea that can occur over the bar is that you may not be able to see the danger until you get close, and this is definitely a case where local knowledge and advice is called for. The harbour master or similar official should be contactable by radio to get an

update on the feasibility of the entrance. Even when the conditions out at sea look relatively calm there can be a ground swell, which out at sea you will hardly notice, but once it approaches shallow water the waves can rear up and break. I have come across this on the east coast of Florida, where a swell from the Atlantic looked totally harmless but when it found the shallows of the river entrance, there were wild breaking seas on a calm day with fog and we had to move on. If you plan to use such a harbour entrance, a call ahead for advice is a must.

This experience reinforces the fact that when you are entering a new harbour it all comes down to planning, so that when you actually enter the harbour you have the resources to cope. Remember to switch your VHF radio to the working channel of the harbour or the marina. You can usually find this information in an almanac or in the pilot guide, and if the harbour and marina have different VHF channels it is a good idea to set up the radio to scan both. The harbour radio will help you to know what is going on inside the harbour, perhaps with information about shipping movements or other activity. From the marina you will hopefully get a berth number, either via the VHF or by means of a call on your mobile phone. It can be a great help to know where you are going to moor before you enter, but not all marina plans show you the berth numbers and you may have to wait until you are actually inside the marina to find your destination.

Tidal issues

In your planning you will want to know what the tide is doing from the point of view of both water depths, if the entrance is shallow, and the direction of the tidal stream. Water depths can be critical in some harbours where there is a large rise and fall of tide, but hopefully you will have timed your arrival to take place when the conditions are favourable for entry. In regions where the tidal range may be 5m (16ft) or more, depths can be more critical because marinas may have a sill across the entrance that maintains the depth inside the

In a crowded harbour the line of the channel may not always be clear.

Channel buoys can often be laid quite close to shoals.

GPS assistance

The electronic chart can help a lot in planning entry into a harbour. These days GPS has an accuracy of possibly around 20m (65ft), which should be enough to plot your position accurately enough all the way into harbour, but there are things you need to consider before relying on GPS positioning. Firstly, how accurate do you need the positioning to be in the particular harbour you are entering? In many harbours the margins can be quite tight, and while 20m sounds very accurate it may not be enough, particularly

when you need to allow some margin of safety outside that 20m limit. Then there is the accuracy of the electronic chart you are using to plot the position. Electronic charts are not necessarily updated at regular intervals and harbour channels can change over the years. Harbour authorities tend to adapt to these changes by moving buoys around so they continue to indicate the channel, but these changes may not show up on your chart.

So yes, GPS can help enormously and should take you close to a marina entrance where visual navigation can take over. It should be accurate enough to get you to the fairway buoy at a harbour entrance, but think carefully about entering if you do not actually see the buoy. Basically you need to use your judgement and remember that GPS is a great help and works extremely well out in the open sea, but harbour navigation, even today, relies heavily on visual navigation and your planning should take this into account.

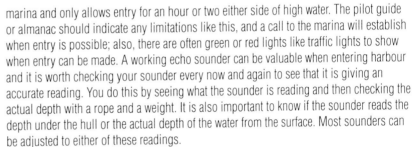

marina and only allows entry for an hour or two either side of high water. The pilot guide or almanac should indicate any limitations like this, and a call to the marina will establish when entry is possible; also, there are often green or red lights like traffic lights to show when entry can be made. A working echo sounder can be valuable when entering harbour and it is worth checking your sounder every now and again to see that it is giving an accurate reading. You do this by seeing what the sounder is reading and then checking the actual depth with a rope and a weight. It is also important to know if the sounder reads the depth under the hull or the actual depth of the water from the surface. Most sounders can be adjusted to either of these readings.

You need to remember that the echo sounder only shows the depth directly underneath the hull, so it will not give advance warning of approaching shallows. You can see the trend as the water gets deeper or shallower, but at what point do you decide you must stop because the shoaling is continuing? There is no easy answer to this and it can be a nervous time when you know there is a bar or a shallow spit across an entrance and you watch the depth getting less and less. This is where you need to have confidence in your calculations and in the chart information if you are planning to cut the margins fine. My advice is not to cut the margins too fine unless you are prepared to take the risk.

Harbour markers

Many harbour entrance channels are marked by buoys and/or leading lights, plus beacons and lighthouses. Each harbour will have its own combination, and remember that these marks are generally laid to aid the navigation of larger ships. Often there is plenty of water for yachts outside the main channel, but tread cautiously here because these areas may not be surveyed regularly. If you stick to the buoyed channel as you come in, you will be safe, and if there is a longish stretch of buoyed channel, mark off the buoys on the chart as you pass them to keep a check on where you are.

Shipping will have priority in harbour channels.

Breaking water on a shoal will act as a warning.

Once you pick up the buoys marking the entrance channel you should have no problem following them, provided you are entering a reasonably sized port. However, your cruising plans may be more adventurous and take you to small out-of-the-way ports where perhaps there is only a series of stakes or withies to mark the channel. If you plan to enter harbours like this, it pays to get some local advice before entering, and often a quick phone call will confirm what you can expect to find in the entrance. There are other harbours, particularly those with a bar, that can shift and change with the weather, where the buoys marking the channel will be moved accordingly. Once again, some local advice can go a long way to help or confirm things before you enter.

Mooring buoys close to the channel can be a hazard to navigation.

Don't be put off by all these cautions – most harbour entrances are straightforward and easy provided you have charts showing the details. Remember that you can always stop and work things out if you are not sure on the way in, although on a strong flood tide this may be harder. There are two schools of thought here. One suggests that entering on the flood tide is best, because then if you should touch bottom, the rising tide will lift the boat and you can carry on; the other says that entering on the ebb tide is better, because then you are stemming the tide and it is easy to stop and hold your position if you want to work out where to go next. There is no easy answer and you must make the decision according to the circumstances. It is best to avoid navigating by feel if you can and while a sailboat keel will not normally suffer damage by touching the bottom, you really do not want to push your luck to this sort of limit and certainly not if there are rocks around.

Switching from sail to motor

Another decision you have to make is the point at which you switch from sail power to motors. Many owners love the challenge of entering harbour under sail and with a competent crew on board there should not be a problem. You definitely do not want even to think about entering a marina under sail so you need to allow time to make the transition from sail to power and to get mooring lines and fenders ready. A brief halt off the entrance of a marina is required to get the sails stowed and the moorings ready; but on a long, winding estuary or river entrance you could continue under sail for some way as long as the wind is favourable.

Tacking up a river channel might look seamanlike and impress onlookers – but it is not likely to impress your crew. A modern sailboat may be able to do 7 knots or more under engine power, so have regard for speed limits in harbours – the excessive wash you might create at full speed will not endear you to other boaters or the authorities. Taking it more slowly also buys you time to work things out.

In summary

Most harbours are very straightforward and well marked so there should be no problems in entering. In preparation, first study the chart carefully. Make a note of critical marks and buoys at turning points in the channel. Look for leading marks that could help to guide you in and confirm that you are indeed in the channel. There are usually so many clues there to help you and you always have the GPS position on the electronic chart as a guide and the echo sounder as confirmation. However, while it can be relatively easy to get confirmation of your position, what can be worrying is when these different sources of information do not line up and you get conflicting information about where you are. My advice then is to rely on visual rather than electronic information, but even with visual information mistakes can be made. The real answer is to prepare thoroughly and be fully alert to all the possibilities. Entering a strange harbour is likely to be one of the more critical aspects of navigation – just don't let this put you off.

Right: Fenders out in good time as long as you know which side will be alongside.

Preparing to berth

You have entered the harbour or the marina safely – now what? If you know the berth you have been allocated, that is fine and you can prepare for coming alongside. Many marinas have a visitor or arrival berth close by the entrance to the marina and if you have not been allocated a berth, this is the place to tie up and talk to the marina staff. Most marinas are pretty organised these days and very efficient at arranging a berth if one is available. Harbours without marinas can be a different story and the harbour authorities may offer you a place to tie up or to pick up a mooring. Finding a space to anchor in any harbour these days is now only a remote possibility because the space is too valuable to have a yacht swinging around an anchor.

It may not be easy to find your allocated berth in a crowded marina.

One of the main dilemmas I have found when entering harbour is that you never seem to know which side of the boat will be alongside until the very last minute. This means that the crew end up with a great rush to get the fenders in place before coming alongside. Even when you know the side for the fenders, getting them at the right height to be effective can be hit and miss. As you approach the berth it can pay to pause for a moment, if conditions allow, while the fenders are sorted out, otherwise you may find your crew so busy with the fenders that they do not have time for the ropes. It can all end in an indecent rush that does not look very seamanlike, so try to buy time for the fenders and ropes before actually coming alongside.

The shiny finish on a modern yacht does need protection from scuffing alongside, so fenders are a must in virtually every case. Cylindrical fenders are best as they offer a bit more height flexibility and will stay in place better than round ones. In most marina berths they stay in place because either the pontoons rise and fall or there is little or no tide to worry about. When you are alongside a fixed jetty or quay where there is a tide rise and fall, fendering can be tricky and you need a vertical section on the quay for the fender to stay in place. Where the jetty is supported by vertical piles the fender will not stay in place where you want it, and one solution is to have a plank that spans the space between the piles for the fender to rest against. It sounds easy but trying to find such a plank can be a challenge. There is no easy answer here and perhaps the best solution is to hang a cylindrical fender horizontally so there is a bit of latitude in its location alongside the pile. If you regularly tie up to jetties or quays with piling, which can happen when you visit the more remote harbours where facilities are limited, it might pay to construct longer fenders that will span the gaps better. Some yachtsmen drop a canvas over the side between the fenders and the hull to reduce the chance of grit scratching the sensitive shiny surface.

Fenders with a canvas backing on the hull to reduce scratching.

✓ Top Tip

'I know this place'

One thing to be careful about is when one of your crew says, 'I know this harbour well, I've been here many times before. Let me take her in.' Forgive me for being a cynic but this sort of local knowledge can be a mixed blessing and I have been aground in the Menai Straits because one of the crew thought they knew the way through the buoyed channel but got confused. When someone offers local knowledge, take it with a pinch of salt. It can be helpful in a fast-changing situation but don't sit back and relax, thinking all is well.

Local knowledge can suddenly run out of steam and you have to take over at short notice, so keep a very careful eye on progress. If you have to do this, you might as well do the navigation anyway; after all, as the skipper, the responsibility is yours.

Guidance from the harbour master can be helpful in locating your berth.

Mooring ropes

If you normally keep your boat in a marina, the chances are you will have relatively short mooring ropes. You don't need long ropes for tying up in a marina and indeed long ropes can be a nuisance and difficult to handle when all you need is something perhaps 10m (33ft) long as a maximum. However, when you are cruising there could be situations where longer ropes are not only desirable but

necessary. If you find yourself having to moor in a harbour where there is a surge in the water from a swell outside, longer ropes absorb the surge more efficiently. With a short span of mooring rope you find the boat tends to jerk and pull on the lines, making life very uncomfortable on board, while the long rope will cope much better.

Then you may have to moor in a berth where there is a range of tide of perhaps 2m (6–7ft) or more. With short ropes out to the quay you will have to constantly adjust the ropes as the boat rises and falls with the tide. Longer ropes led well forward and aft will cope with the rise and fall much better and hopefully you can get a good night's sleep. One final point about longer ropes: if you ever have to tow with your boat or be towed, a longer rope will

It is best to double up on the mooring line when tied to a buoy.

absorb the shock loadings involved in towing much better than a shorter rope, so at least a couple of longer ropes, perhaps 30m (100ft) long or even longer, should be part of your cruising kit.

Some fairleads are barely adequate for their job.

Mediterranean moorings

The berths in marinas tend to be two distinct types. There is the common type of berth in the Mediterranean, where you back in stern first with ropes onto the quay from the stern and ropes from the bow connected to a pre-laid anchor or mooring. In some of these so-called Mediterranean moorings you may have to use your own anchor to hold the bow, dropping it as you back into the berth. This requires careful judgement to get it in the right place and it needs to be as close as possible directly out from the berth you are backing into. However, most Mediterranean marinas these days have ropes laid in place that you pick up from the quay and carry forward as the bow rope.

Yachts on Mediterranean moorings in harbour.

Because these ropes run from ahead of the bow back to the quay it is very easy to get them tangled round your propeller when they are being lifted, so care is needed about using the propellers, both when the ropes are being lifted into place and when they are being let go. You need to get the ropes in place as quickly as possible to hold the stern away from the quay and because you have to use the engines for this until the bow rope is fast, those ropes and the propellers can come into close proximity. At least by using pre-laid ropes you will not have the problem of fouling your anchor with that of the boat in the next berth. It can become a real cat's cradle of anchors and chains with closely laid moorings and cause considerable delays when it comes to departing if each yacht has to use its own anchor.

Aids to berthing

Backing into a berth with the single engine of a sailboat requires skill and judgement and an azimuthing sail drive is a huge benefit as it can be used for sideways thrust. The bow thruster is also a valuable tool for tight manoeuvring and some yachts are now being fitted with a 'point and go' joystick that takes a lot of the guesswork out of close-quarters manoeuvring. Here you just point the joystick in the direction you want the boat to go and the amount by which you move it dictates the speed on movement. Sailboats with a deep

Outboard engines

Small sailboats might have a long shaft outboard as the auxiliary engine and here the propeller gives not only the forward thrust but also the steering thrust – unless of course the outboard is fixed and you use the yacht's rudder for steering. Steering thrust with an outboard is only available when the propeller is turning so don't expect steering control once you have taken the engine out of gear. However, you do still have steering control from the yacht's rudder so you might want to use a combination of these when trying to manoeuvre into a berth.

Chafing

I am always surprised at the number of new boats coming onto the market that have fairleads with sharp edges. The whole purpose of fairleads on boats is to give a rope a smooth path over or through the side of the boat so the rope will not chafe. The fairleads on many boats today seem to be designed more as a fashion statement than a practical piece of equipment.

If the boat is moored in a marina where there is no appreciable movement in the water, these modern fairleads might be adequate, but even when you step on board the boat moves and the mooring ropes move, so chafe could result. Chafe is a longer-term problem where a boat may be left for a week or two and it moves, perhaps up and down with the tide or when a swell comes into the harbour. In a worst-case scenario a rope could chafe right through, but in most cases the rope will only be weakened and rendered unfit for purpose. Rope is not a cheap item but a bit of care can prolong its life considerably.

Simply tying a piece of rag around the rope where it passes through the fairlead will help, but it does not look very pretty. A better solution is to split a short length of plastic tubing, slip it over the rope and hold it in place with small lashings

at either end. A similar solution can be used when you are tied up to a mooring buoy, but here you will also need to look for chafe and sort out protection at the point where the rope passes through the eye on the buoy.

Top: This buoy mooring lines has anti-chafe covering at the fairlead.

Centre left: A sharp edged fairlead will soon start to chafe a mooring rope.

Centre right: A bow fender could reduce damage when a yacht is moored bow into a pontoon.

keel are not too affected by the wind when manoeuvring because they have a good 'bite' on the water, but the wind can affect centreboard and bilge keel cruisers. Be aware that joystick controls may not have enough sideways thrust to counter the pressure of the wind on the hull in a strong breeze.

Sailboats usually have large rudders and excellent steering control and you can use this for harbour manoeuvring. Even at slow speed this rudder control can be effective and it is even more so if you just give a quick burst ahead on the throttle, when the boat will turn while making little or no headway. This feature can be particularly useful when backing into a berth without the benefit of thrusters and that quick kick ahead on the engine with the rudder hard over can be used to straighten up the yacht if it gets a bit out of line. The steering effect of the rudder when going astern is usually quite limited and will only be effective when the yacht has some way on her, which you don't usually want in close-quarters manoeuvring.

Finger piers

The other type of marina berth is the one that has finger piers extending out from the main pontoon. These can look quite fragile and may only extend out for perhaps half the length of your yacht, but they work well although you need to think carefully about how to lay out your mooring ropes when using them, as it is not possible to fit a bow rope leading ahead. In this case the stern spring holds the stern away from the pontoon with a bow spring to stop the boat moving ahead. It is a bit like mooring in reverse, but think about how you need to hold the boat in position and it is quite easy to work out what you need. Always think of at least four ropes out when you moor up, two leading forward and two astern, so the boat is not only held securely in place but there is a bit of redundancy if one rope should break or otherwise come undone.

If the boat is being left in the berth for any length of time, check out the mooring ropes for the potential to chafe. So often fairleads and cleats are designed for style rather than practicality, so put some waste material between the rope and the fairlead if your fittings have sharp edges. Most fairleads have an open slot in the top to allow the rope to be slotted in but if the rope has to lead upwards to a quay mooring post these fairleads may not always hold the rope in place. There is not a lot you can do about the fairlead so you need to consider the rope layout carefully and perhaps tie the ropes in place. This can be a problem when the boat is rising and falling with the tide when alongside.

In most harbours all the good places are taken by moorings so finding an anchorage can be very difficult.

Mooring buoys

Picking up a mooring in a harbour can be pretty straightforward and if this is your choice, or all that is on offer, the harbour authorities will probably have allocated you a specific buoy. Buoys are usually numbered but finding yours is never easy and any guidance is always helpful, so don't be afraid to ask.

There are two main types of mooring buoys: those where you put your ropes directly through the eye on the top of the buoy and those where you pick up the buoy and tie up to the section of chain underneath. The latter connects you directly to the mooring chain while the former relies on the buoy itself as the mooring point.

Buoys may have a tail rope attached with a small buoy on the end that makes it easier to pick up, rather than trying to lift the main buoy. You may be able to reach down to the buoy from your bow to pass a rope through the eye, or you may need to launch the tender or get assistance. The rope going through the eye on the buoy can be subject to chafe and you might feel inclined to shackle the rope in place, but then you need to get down there to unshackle when you leave. If you shackle on a rope in this way, always mouse or secure the shackle pin so it won't come unscrewed. It is also wise always to put two ropes onto the buoy so that if one has a problem, you will not be cast adrift.

Top: A double line onto the mooring is good but (top right) a chain is better.

Bottom left: Mooring ropes like this can be an alternative if the anchor occupies the bow lead.

Bottom right: If you are picking up moorings then the tender is a vital piece of equipment.

Rafting up

At busy times in harbours you may be asked to double up, or raft up as it is often known, which means that two or more boats are on the same mooring or in the same berth. If you are first in the berth or at the mooring, you have the job of fendering alongside or securing the mooring. All the second boat has to do is tie up alongside, but to be secure it makes sense not to rely on the first boat's moorings but to run your own ropes to the quay or to the buoy. You need good fendering when you raft up in this way, particularly if there is any movement in the water, and on an overnight stay you might not get the most restful of nights as the two or more boats ride alongside each other with different motions. Rafting up would not be my chosen method of harbour mooring, but at busy times there may be no choice.

'...You need good fendering when you raft up.'

Left: Rafting up becomes necessary in crowded harbours and demands good fendering.

It is mainly sailboats that use moorings – powerboats tend to like marinas.

Anchoring

There are still harbours where you can anchor for the night and if this is your choice, then finding a suitable spot can be tricky. The best spots always go first and you will not make any friends if you try to squeeze into an already crowded anchorage. Anchoring requires space, at least twice the length of the chain you have put out, and when finding a spot you need to consider your distance from other boats, the distance from the shore, and the distance from shallows, bearing in mind with the latter that the area of shallow water can change as the tide rises and falls. So anchoring is hungry on harbour space, which is why it is not encouraged these days; but it usually offers a free berth for the night, so you can see the attraction. Most anchorages in harbours are a long way from the shore and facilities, so by all means try; but don't be disappointed if you end up in the back of nowhere. Anchoring requires considerable seamanship and judgement to get it right and tying up alongside for the night is so much easier.

Before you relax…

When you are safely tied up or moored, there are a couple of points to remember. If you have told someone where you are heading on your cruise that day as a safeguard, do remember to phone in and let them know you have arrived, otherwise they may report you missing. This applies particularly if you have checked in with the Coastguard on departure, then they can tick you off their list. The other necessity is a visit to the marina or the harbour office to pay your dues for the overnight stay. Not only does this save a visit in the morning before departure but it is also a matter of courtesy, which will help if you want to visit again. It may be a condition of using a marina that you have at least third party insurance and if so the marina authorities may want to see proof of this, so do carry your certificate of insurance with you. Harbour and marina authorities have considerable powers these days and they often have a difficult job to do, so keeping things sweet will pay off in the long run.

Above: Drying out after a rough passage.

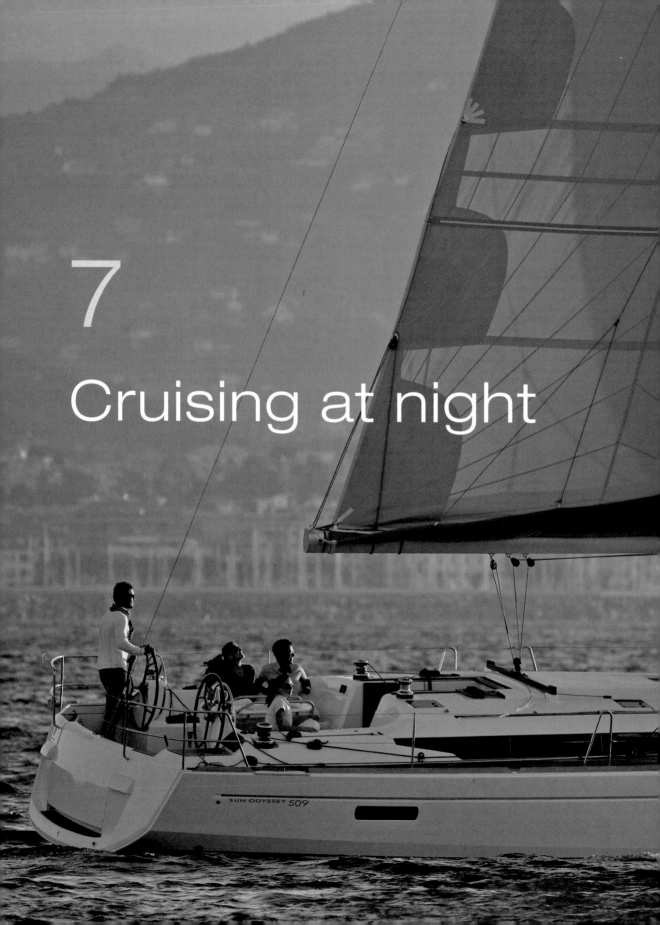

7
Cruising at night

Night navigation

You've cut your cruising teeth on making day cruises along the coasts and have built up experience. Now you feel that the time is ripe for a more challenging cruise, which could include an overnight passage in order to arrive at your destination at dawn. Night navigation brings new challenges to both the planning and the navigation and both require a new approach. When you are out at sea at night, gone is the nice familiar scene of land and buoys and other navigation marks that can help you with the visual navigation. In daylight you can see what the wind and waves are doing and pick out any floating debris and small craft. At night all this is replaced by fixed and flashing lights that you need to decipher before you can understand what they are and what sort of threat they may offer to challenge your progress. Of course the electronic systems and the GPS will still work in the same way and there is a tendency to rely on these much more heavily at night; the same applies to the wind instruments, because it is not easy to see just which way the wind is blowing and how the sails are setting. A visual navigation check is still a vital element at night to ensure a safe passage, but it is lights rather than features that provide the clues.

Planning for a night passage

Like everything else to do with cruising, planning is the key to success in night navigation. Not only do you need to plot the course and the waypoints to take you to your destination, you also need to look at the chart to see what lights and signals you might pass on the way. I find the paper chart a great help with night navigation because it has all the light characteristics already shown, while with the electronics you have to click on the buoy or light to open up a box that shows the light characteristics and details. There are some clever electronics coming into use that actually show the light of a buoy flashing on the display not only with its proper sequence but also in colour, and this can help a lot at night; but it is also distracting. Trying to view a paper chart at night can be difficult because of the small print and the need to avoid bright lights, and I solve this problem by writing the light characteristics of a buoy or lighthouse alongside it in large letters so I have a quick reference either when I am looking out for the next flashing light or when I see

Below left: Sunset is the time to switch into night mode and check that everything on board is secure.

Below right: The moon can often give you enough light at night to pick out land features.

Top Tip

Cracking the night-time code

Instead of the quick and easy interpretation of what you see around you in daylight, at night everything you see outside the cockpit is in code. You have to translate this code into meaningful navigation lights and the lights of shipping, and all this can happen against a confusing background of shore lights. The first time you embark on a night cruise can be daunting, but it is also exciting and rewarding. The deciphering work can add to the workload of the navigator at a time when he may already be under pressure from operating the boat in the new environment of darkness. Night navigation and operations can be challenging but there are ways to simplify things if you get organised.

a flashing light on the horizon. One of the problems with using electronic charts is that you cannot tailor or annotate them to your own requirements and you are stuck with what the system's designer decides you should have. One day the manufacturers will wake up to the requirements of the practical navigator, and I would very much like to be able to annotate the electronic chart with the additional information I need.

So I like to use a combination of electronic and paper charts to navigate with at night – handling paper charts in the open cockpit is not easy, so the emphasis tends to be on the electronics. That bright screen in front of you at the helm provides a lot of good information, although it tempts you to focus on the screen rather than what is going on around you outside the boat. Before the advent of electronic help you had to rely almost entirely on flashing navigation lights to find out where you were, plotting bearings on the paper chart. You would tend to focus on finding out where you were rather than on where you were going and this added to the pressure of night navigation. Today the job of navigating at night is made much easier by modern electronics. The electronic chart will show you precisely where you are and, perhaps more important, where you are going.

The radar should identify any boats and ships that are around and will also give you a reassuring view of the land features as they come up. AIS can even tell you the type of ship or boat and the destination of many of the targets you see on the radar. You could argue that navigating at night is the ultimate test of electronic navigation because you will be putting a lot more faith in the electronic systems than you might in the daytime. This faith can be justified to a certain extent, but as always with navigation it is very reassuring to get confirmation from a visual check that all is going according to plan.

The basic method of navigating at night is very much the same as navigation in daylight. You do your passage planning and work out the course you want to follow on either the paper or electronic chart, you mark the waypoints where the course will be altered, and you check the route in detail to ensure you are not passing close to or even over the top of any dangers. Checking the course on the chart is particularly important when you are using electronics because some of the inshore details might not be shown on some of the larger scales you might use for route planning,

You can see some amazing sunrises after a night at sea.

So planning for a night passage should include not only the electronic plot but also what you can expect to see visually. You can pick up buoy lights perhaps 2 or 3 miles away while lighthouses can have a range of up to 20 miles, although weaker ones might be as little as 5 miles away before you see them. Distant lighthouses can cause some confusion because you don't expect to see them flashing such a long way away and tend to be focusing on the nearby navigation lights. Coloured lights, which are usually red on a coloured lighthouse light but can be green or red on a buoy, will not show up at the same range as a white light, and these coloured lights can be very difficult to pick out if there are brighter lights around. Occulting lights, where the light is on more than off, can be particularly difficult to spot, while the quick flashing ones are the easiest to see.

You can find many vessels without lights in a harbour at night.

Autopilot

Probably the best piece of electronic equipment you can have on board for a night passage is the autopilot. Not only does it relieve you of the job of steering the boat and give you more time to attend to the navigation and identify the flashing lights, but it also stabilises the view of both the outside world and the radar display, if you have one. If you are hand-steering, you have to focus on the compass at night as the main heading reference, which can result in the boat swinging about as you steer. This can make it hard to indentify lights, both the fixed lights of shipping and the flashing lights of buoys. Because of their intermittent appearance, the flashing lights can pose a particular problem to identify if they are moving around the horizon as the boat's heading changes. You will watch for them at the point where you thought they first appeared, only to find they have shifted 10° or 20° to one side or the other while you were momentarily concentrating on the steering. You will have a job to pick them out and sort out which light is which as the boat's head swings around. With the autopilot doing its job of keeping the boat on a steady heading, everything will be more stable and lights will appear where you expect them to be, making navigation a lot easier.

Sunrise can bring welcome relief after a night passage.

The radar display will also be stabilised by using the autopilot, giving you a much better and more useable picture. Most small boat radars have a relative display, which means that the display is shown with the boat's head at the top and all the targets are shown relative to the boat's heading; so, for example, a ship on the port bow will show up on the display as a target on the port bow, which makes for easy and logical interpretation. Whatever the heading of the boat, the heading line on the radar will always run up to the top of the display, so if the boat's heading is swinging about, the targets on the display will swing about to the same degree and be that much harder to track. With the stabilised display you get when the autopilot is holding the boat's heading more or less stable, the buoys, the land, and other boats and ships will stay more or less in the same place on the screen, making it much easier to relate them to what you see outside, and it will be much easier to judge their relative motion.

Adapting the navigation plan

Now you have the basics of the navigation plan in place, this is the time to adapt it to make night-time navigation easier and safer. A first step here is to look along the route to see which points of land or navigation marks will be identifiable at night. These points will provide you with that vital visual confirmation that the electronic systems are giving you reliable information. Don't be tempted to rely totally on the electronics – you should constantly be looking at ways to obtain a visual check on the navigation situation.

The lights on navigation marks are obviously the best for this checking. Even these days, when the number of lights is being cut back, there are still enough left out there for you always to have one in sight when navigating along a coastline. You may lose them on an open sea passage, such as across the English Channel, but later you will pick up the lights on the other shore. The challenge in your navigation planning is to make best use of these lights to help you check out the electronics.

You might also want to adjust the courses you set to make life easier at night. Rather than take the direct route between waypoints, you might find it beneficial to take a course that passes close to a buoy or other mark with a light. This will give you a positive position check as you pass. If you are steering manually, having a light ahead or nearly ahead to steer on is also much easier than trying to steer a compass course. Do not try to steer directly towards a light, partly because other boats may be doing the same thing but also because it is not easy to judge distances at night and you can find yourself much closer to the buoy than you intended to be. I can recollect times when approaching a buoy at night to find myself suddenly almost on top of it, and with the tide setting me down onto it. It can be particularly hard to judge your distance from a flashing buoy light, so make sure that the bearing of the buoy is opening up as you get closer to be certain that you will pass clear. If the bearing stays the same, you are on a collision course with the buoy and you need to make a change of course.

Caution at night

When cruising at night, you are guided mainly by lights and electronics. Unless there is bright moonlight you will not be able to assess the sea conditions, and there are many other things you will not see. Therefore it pays to be more cautious at night, and allow wider passing margins and not sail too close to the wind.

At night you will not see any debris floating in the water and there is not much you can do about that. In my experience it is not a serious problem and I have no recollection of hitting anything at night that caused damage or even an impact on the hull. You will not be able to see any lobster pots or other fishing gear either, but you should be able to avoid those by keeping further offshore than you would in daylight – perhaps a minimum of 2 miles off, but there are no guarantees.

You will not see any wash from passing ships that could upset your smooth running, but you will see the lights of passing ships so you can anticipate and be ready for any wash that might come along. Such a wash is only likely to be disturbing if you are fairly close, and any ship passing more than, say, a mile off should not pose a problem.

You will also not see any tide races or other disturbed water until you enter it, but these areas can be anticipated to a certain extent as detailed in the chapter on weather, so it should not be difficult to take avoiding action.

You will be less aware of squalls and gusts approaching because you will not see the telltale visual signs, so it might be sensible to run with a reduced sail area at night. You might need particular caution when running before the wind to avoid a gybe in any wind shift; and I would certainly hesitate to fly a spinnaker at night unless you have a strong crew.

Big ships at night can move very fast compared with a sailing yacht.

It can be hard to see approaching storms and squalls at night unless there is lightning.

Navigation lights

A quick glance around the horizon is not enough for a good lookout at night. Flashing lights only show up at intervals so you will need a slow scan of the horizon if you are to pick them up. Be aware that the sails might blanket visibility over some sectors, so frequent looking out to leeward is a good idea. Again, a quick scan is not enough because the small, faint lights that might indicate a small boat close by will only become apparent when you concentrate on the lookout. Not all targets will show up on the radar, particularly if there is some sea clutter at the centre of the screen, and small boats are not required to have very bright navigation lights so from a distance they can look like glow worms. The requirements for navigation lights at night are far from perfect and a single white light could mean many things – a stern light, a small boat, an anchor light, or just a boat's working light. You can be quite close before you see a weak light so constant vigilance is vital, particularly in crowded waters, and you need time to crack the code of the lights you see at sea at night.

You also need to consider your own navigation lights. It is easy to switch them on and assume that other craft will see you clearly at night, but some boatbuilders look to cut costs where possible and there is little incentive to fit bright lights when a cheaper, less bright light will meet the regulations. Sailboats are only required to show the red and green navigation lights forward and a stern light aft, and from another vessel these can be very hard to pick out, particularly when they are viewed against a shoreline with lights. When I am at sea I want to be seen at night as much as possible so I consider that good bright navigation lights are essential, particularly in busy waters. Bright navigation lights might take more power from the limited battery supply but they are a good investment. Keep a powerful torch handy as well, so that you can shine it on the sails if other vessels get close and appear not to have seen you. I like the idea of fitting a very bright strobe light at the masthead, which you can switch on if other vessels get close, but this is not allowed by the COLREGs and might cause confusion.

Having poor navigation lights is rather like driving your car at night with only the sidelights on. A small boat with poor lights might not be sighted until less than a mile away and it can be even more difficult when there are shore lights behind the target boat.

Right: Make sure that your navigation lights are in order for night sailing.

Far right: Your navigation lights can be little more than a glow-worm to other vessels.

Identifying boats and navigation lights against shore lighting can be a considerable challenge, made worse as the shore lighting gets brighter and there are flashing neon signs and even pedestrian crossing beacons to add to the confusion. When you have seen a buoy light or a boat against this background you can often lose sight of it again unless you concentrate hard, and even big ships can seemingly disappear against a background of shore lights because their lights appear high up when the ships are close and you tend to be more focused on the horizon than looking upwards. Navigating through the Straits of Messina was a nightmare at night, with shore lights on both sides of the Strait, shipping passing through, and busy ferries crossing. The radar can be a great help in identifying the relative movement of vessels and lights, but you really need to keep on your toes in this sort of situation to avoid coming close to other vessels, and it is wise to have the engine either running or at least ready to start quickly if you need to take quick avoiding action. You can keep inshore to avoid much of the traffic, but then you may come up against small fishing boats.

The single white light can be particularly hard to detect in these conditions and even when you pick one up it can be very difficult to judge its distance. If it is the stern light of a boat in front, it may be moving at or near the same speed as you, and because its relative position does not change much it can be easily lost against any background lights. The radar can be an enormous help in giving you a plan view of what is around you and the relative movements of other vessels, but it will not pick up all small craft. If you are the only person on watch at night, you will have a full time job in this sort of situation. You have to keep the lookout, scanning the horizon for lights; you have to monitor the navigation and radar; and you may have to steer the boat if you are not under autopilot. In crowded waters, you do need at least two people on watch in these situations. The temptation will always be to focus on the electronic screens because these are the most interesting things in view. There is no doubt they will give you much of the information you need for navigating the boat safely, but there is no guarantee that they will show everything that is out there.

Night vision

An important aspect of keeping a good lookout at night is maintaining your 'night vision'. This means dimming the electronic screens and the cabin lights, if the door is open. If you have the engine running, then dashboard lights might need dimming, and there will be lights from instruments like the autopilot to contend with. The electronic screens are the worst offenders these days because they are waterproof and can be installed in the cockpit. Here you need to find a balance between convenience and practicality and decide what you need in the cockpit and what can be installed below at the chart table.

It is worth spending some time getting your boat helm organised for night-time operations. Make sure you know how to dim the navigation screens, and work out where reflections and light sources might obstruct your view. I know from experience that you can spend some time trying to sort out these errant lights at night after you have gone to sea, but you could get many of them sorted out in harbour before you leave. It is useful to have electronics where the control buttons are illuminated at night because it can be frustrating if you have to get a torch out every time you want to alter a setting on the display. Not only does this take your mind off the navigation but the light of the torch will also temporarily destroy your night vision – although the control illumination itself can be irritating at

Demands on energy

The demands on your battery can be heavy at night, particularly if you have an autopilot in operation. This replaces the normal manual steering with a form of power steering that puts a considerable drain on the battery. Then there are the electronics, the navigation lights and probably some cabin lights to power, as well as the normal domestic things like the fridge. You can always top up the battery by running the engine and if you have a wind or towed generator that will help too. Of course, solar panels will not work at night, so if you rely on this you will need to keep a close eye on the remaining battery power. A low battery only adds to the increased stress of night navigation, so plan how you will maintain battery capacity before you leave harbour.

There can be distinctive lights or features that can help you enter harbour at night.

night. One of the critical controls that you definitely want illuminated is the autopilot standby switch, which you will need to find in a hurry when you want to disconnect the autopilot and revert the steering to manual control.

Rather than have the full screen fixed electronic screen switched on in the cockpit at night, a portable GPS and chart unit kept in your pocket might be an option so that you just pull it out when required. It won't offer radar but it can be a useful guide.

Avoiding collisions at night

For collision avoidance at night, you need to know the COLREGs and have a clear understanding of what all the different lights mean.

You need first of all to know what the lights on the other ship indicate, and as long as the vessel has sidelights as well as the masthead lights you can get a pretty fair idea of how the other vessel is heading by their relative positions. However, you will not get the same precise heading of another vessel that you can in daylight, when you can actually see it, so in order to establish whether a risk of collision exists you need to watch the bearing of the other vessel and see how it changes. Provided your boat is running under autopilot and has a steady heading, you may be able to see the bearing changing visually. Alternatively you can put the bearing cursor of the radar onto the target and then see how the target changes in relation to the cursor line. If it moves significantly aft of the cursor line, you can be confident that there is no risk of collision and that you can maintain your course and speed; and if the target moves significantly ahead of the line, you also know there is no risk of collision. Where you need to watch out is when there is little or no change in the bearing.

The COLREGs give sailboats a considerable element of priority over other vessels, but this assumes firstly that they have seen you and secondly that they are aware you are a sailing boat. Don't take anything for granted in this respect and always err on the side of caution and be defensive. Other vessels may easily overestimate your speed and underestimate your limitations of manoeuvre, so having the engine ready for starting is a good safety

Right: You need to know what all the ship's navigation lights mean at night.

feature. The COLREGs are complex and a full understanding is important, particularly at night when it is not so easy to work out just how the other vessel is heading. If you do act defensively and decide to take avoiding action, make sure you take it early, and also work on the assumption that the other vessel may not have seen you – a very cautious approach is best in any potential collision situation. The next chapter on fog navigation will look at this in more depth.

Entering harbour

So you need planning before you start, you need an organised cockpit, and you need concentration when you are navigating at night. However, the most challenging part of the job at night will be entering harbour.

A big lighthouse at a harbour entrance should show up well against the shore lights and give you a guide to find the entrance channel. However, it can be a real struggle to pick out a buoy light against the shore lights. Once you have found the first fairway buoy it will be easier to locate the others against the shore lights because you will have some idea where to look. The electronic chart can be very valuable when entering harbour at night because the GPS should be accurate enough to position you in the entrance channel and show a plan view of an unfamiliar harbour. Don't rely on it completely, but it can help considerably to sort out the various features of the harbour in the confusion of the dark, and it is a great aid to help you get the spatial positioning you need in a strange harbour.

Entering harbour at night

Entering harbour at night can be a challenging experience, even when the harbour is relatively familiar. The main problem stems from the difficulty in picking up the harbour navigation lights, especially against a background of shore lights and flashing neon signs, but identifying other harbour features can also create problems.

The first step in entering a harbour at night is preparation. Study the chart carefully and in detail so that you build up a mental picture of what it might look like. Many electronic chart systems allow you to see an actual picture of the harbour but of course these are daylight images and may not be so helpful for night entry. Note the light characteristics of the buoys in the harbour and, if you have a choice,

enter harbour against the ebb tide so that you have time to stop and work things out when you are not sure.

It is in these circumstances that the electronic chart really comes into its own. Modern cartography shows the harbour features in considerable detail and you should be able to rely on the GPS position on the electronic chart to an accuracy of 20 metres; but be aware that in a steep-sided harbour you could suffer a temporary loss of GPS positioning. Electronic chart positioning should be used as a guide rather than the primary means of navigation.

One of the major problems in entering a harbour at night lies in identifying other vessels in the harbour. The fixed lights

of these vessels will not always show up well against the shore lights, particularly when the vessels are slow-moving or at anchor, and the masthead-mounted white lights of other sailboats when under motor can be particularly difficult to see. Radar set on a short range can help here, particularly to pick out any shipping in the harbour.

Lights in harbours can present a confusing picture at night.

Night navigation factors

- Using the autopilot can reduce the workload and keep a steadier course.

- Always check the electronic positions with visual checks when possible.

- Have the characteristics of navigation lights readily available before you start out.

- Remember it can be difficult to judge distances at night.

- Electronics can help a lot but do not rely on them totally, particularly radar.

- Spotting the lights of other yachts against the shore lights can be difficult.

- The drain on the battery can be heavier at night, so watch out for this and recharge if necessary/possible.

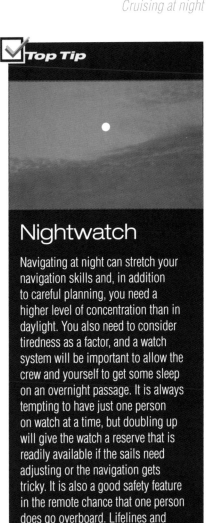

✓ Top Tip

Nightwatch

Navigating at night can stretch your navigation skills and, in addition to careful planning, you need a higher level of concentration than in daylight. You also need to consider tiredness as a factor, and a watch system will be important to allow the crew and yourself to get some sleep on an overnight passage. It is always tempting to have just one person on watch at a time, but doubling up will give the watch a reserve that is readily available if the sails need adjusting or the navigation gets tricky. It is also a good safety feature in the remote chance that one person does go overboard. Lifelines and lifejackets can be a good idea even when in the cockpit at night.
In return for the extra work and planning involved, you will get a great sense of achievement when you make harbour after a successful night passage.

The light of the moon can add a new dimension to night navigation.

8
Cruising in fog

The curse of going to sea

Poor visibility is the curse of going to sea. It is akin to going blind and your cruising world changes dramatically. You can plan for and cope with strong winds because they tend to be forecast well in advance, but poor visibility is much harder to forecast and can have a major impact on your ability to undertake cruising. Fortunately, it tends to be much less prevalent during the summer months, usually the time for serious cruising, so it may not have a major impact on your plans – but if it does happen you may have to make some short-term decisions, and if you are already out at sea, the pressure to navigate safely to port is quite high. At night your ability to see what is around you can be severely restricted, but at least you are able to see navigation lights, buoy lights and lights on other vessels. In poor visibility even these aids do not work, and to a large extent you are navigating blind. Modern electronics work wonders in assisting you to navigate safely through fog, but even they can only do so much and do not make you 100 per cent safe.

However, the ability to check the information that the electronics produce is still vital to give the peace of mind every navigator craves. It is possible to make a landfall using radar and electronic position fixing, but there is always a considerable sigh of relief when the land is actually sighted if visibility is poor. When it comes to entering or leaving harbour, you are pushing the capabilities of electronics to the limits if you have to do this in poor visibility. In almost everything we do at sea, good visibility is critical for keeping good safety margins, so when visibility is seriously reduced the pressure is on. In fog, caution is the watchword; but before we go into the techniques of coping with poor visibility, let us look at the various causes. Understanding these will better enable you to cope with fog and make wise decisions.

Ships tend to keep going at full speed in fog these days, relying entirely on their radar.

Right: You need intense concentration when navigating in fog.

Forecasting visibility

Despite the importance of estimating visibility, it is one of the hardest parts of the weather forecaster's job. This is particularly the case out at sea, where a limited number of weather reports are generated by reporting stations, or by ships themselves. Many reporting stations are now automatic, so there may be no actual reports of the current visibility in their locality because it is difficult to measure this without human assistance. Also, the conditions that reduce visibility are often the result of quite critical and localised conditions and only a small change in temperatures and wind direction can make the difference between good visibility and bad visibility. To make the situation even more complicated, there can be a number of different reasons for reduced visibility, among them being various types of mist or fog, rain, drizzle, snow and so on, all of which affect visibility to a greater or lesser degree and all of which tend to make life very difficult for both the weather forecaster and the navigator.

Even when it is possible to predict that visibility will be reduced because of the conditions reported in the forecast, these can be quite local in nature or extent, and one of the hardest jobs of the forecaster is to take local conditions into account while producing a general weather forecast. For instance, a forecaster may suggest that there will be rain showers, which will almost certainly reduce visibility for a time; but how can you as a seaman determine whether you are going to have these showers in your immediate locality and whether they are going to pass between you and the land or out to sea? It can be equally difficult to establish where fog and mist will strike, as the conditions necessary for fog or mist to form rely mainly on quite small temperature variations that can change from one mile to the next. It is easier to forecast poor visibility when the conditions are such that large areas will be affected, such as an extensive band of rain with the passage of a front, or where the conditions are so positively in favour of fog developing that the fog banks will be widespread.

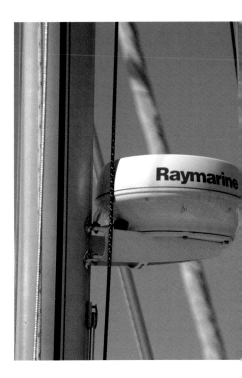

Radar is a vital tool when navigating in fog but you must understand how to interpret it.

These are the clear-cut scenarios that make the forecaster's life easier, and at the other extreme are the obviously clear conditions when the risks of poor visibility are minimal and the forecaster can be equally positive. It's the bits in between that provide the challenge, for example, when there is rain light enough not to impair visibility too seriously or when there are showers or intermittent rain or snow where the visibility range could vary with both time and position. However, clues such as 'patches' in the forecasting term 'coastal fog patches' suggest that the fog may be intermittent in nature, although such a forecast will not tell you where those fog patches will occur. This is where you have to take over from the forecaster and try to make an assessment of the local potential for visibility limits, just as you have to in trying to fine-tune the wind and sea forecasts to get a better idea of what is likely to happen in your locality.

How fog is formed

In order to do this, we need to look at how the various types of fog are formed, where rain can be expected to reduce visibility, and where drizzle may be found within particular weather patterns. As with most things that affect the weather, proximity to the land can often have a profound effect on whether visibility is reduced or not. Fog is particularly insidious in this respect in that it is much more likely to form in areas just where you need the best possible visibility in order to navigate safely, such as in harbour or river entrances where critical temperature differences are more likely to occur.

There are two main types of fog found at sea. One is radiation fog, generally formed as the result of the cooling of the land at night. Although it is essentially a land-based fog, it often drifts out to sea in coastal and estuary waters. The second type is advection fog, which is often called a sea fog and is formed by warm moist air blowing in over colder water. For both these types of fog, particular sets of conditions are necessary for the fog to form. Before we look at these in more detail, it is worth considering exactly what fog is.

There is no difference between fog and mist except one of degree, and the actual causes of the reduction in visibility are exactly the same in both cases. In meteorological terms, fog is any reduction in visibility below 1km or half a sea mile and mist is any reduction in visibility above this figure with a top visibility limit of 1 mile. With visibility of half a mile you should not have any major problems in navigating safely but when it gets down to, say, 400m (440yds) or less, you really have to start concentrating.

Radiation fog starting to lift as the sun warms the land.

Radiation fog

Radiation or 'ground' fog occurs when the land cools at night-time and air coming into contact with the cold surface is cooled below its dew point, or the point at which the water vapour in the air will condense and form fog. Although radiation fog forms over the land, it often drifts out to sea, but will usually disperse when it comes into contact with a comparatively warm water surface, generally no more than a mile or two offshore. Radiation fog can extend up to 10 miles off the coast in extreme circumstances, but this is the exception rather than the rule, and I have seen it a few times in river mouths where the colder river water comes into contact with warmer moist air at sea. Radiation fog tends to be associated with the type of conditions prevailing in anticyclones or areas of high pressure. These weather patterns provide the clear skies and light winds necessary for the initial formation of the fog.

Types of fog

Type of fog and season	Areas affected	Factors for formation	Factors for dispersal
RADIATION FOG (usually October to March)	Inland and harbour areas, particularly where the surrounding land is low-lying and moist	Cooling due to radiation from the ground on clear nights when the wind is light – usually a feature of anticyclone weather	Dispersed when the sun's heat warms the ground or by an increase in the wind strength
ADVECTION FOG (usually spring and early summer when seas are still cool)	Sea and adjacent coasts, and may penetrate into harbours; also open seas where cold waters exist	Cooling of warmer moist air when it comes into contact with the cooler seas	Usually disperses when the wind direction changes and it can also be dispersed near coasts when the sun warms the land/sea
FRONTAL FOG (at all seasons)	Mainly over high ground and occasionally at sea	Lowering of the cloud base along the line of a frontal system	Dispersed when the front passes through

In temperate climates, radiation or ground fog is generally a feature of autumn and winter weather because during these periods the air tends to be moist and the nights are long, which allows for more extensive cooling. For radiation fog to clear it needs the warmth of the sun to raise the temperature of both the air and the land so that the air temperature rises above the dew point, at which point the water vapour will condense. In winter, when the sun's rays are generally weak and there is only limited heating power, radiation fog can be slow to clear and can persist right throughout the day, getting thicker again as night falls. In a period of settled anticyclone conditions it is possible for radiation fog to persist for several days during the winter. Radiation fog tends to start just before or just after dawn, when night temperatures are at their lowest and the wind is at a minimum or even dies away completely. As a general rule, the maximum intensity of radiation fog is found about an hour after sunrise, while the minimum intensity, if the fog has persisted all day, is likely to be in the early afternoon.

Radiation fog has a lot of local effects and there are some particular areas where the fog is much more likely to occur than others. One of these is in the vicinity of industrial areas and large cities, where smoke pollution introduces particulates into the air that can aid the formation of the fog. Radiation fog is also more pronounced in sheltered areas, because here the cooling of the land at night tends to be more pronounced than in places that are exposed to the wind. However, such sheltered areas are less likely to be found along the coast, and as far as the seaman is concerned a more sinister effect is found in valleys and low-lying ground, where colder air formed over higher land tends to roll down into the valley and then out to sea as a bank of fog.

A characteristic of radiation fog is that it is usually very shallow in depth because only the air in contact with or close to the ground is cooled sufficiently for the water vapour to condense. These conditions can produce weird effects where you can see higher ground and buildings but not the sea surface. A high bridge might show up clearly but at sea level below there may be visibility of less than 100m (110yds). In most cases the fog will burn up as the sun rises, and if this fog develops when you are cruising, you may want to consider delaying your departure for an hour or two. Alternatively, you may feel brave enough to feel your way out of the harbour in the hope of finding a clearance when you get to sea.

Advection fog

Advection fog is formed when warm, moist air passes over a cold surface (when the sea provides this cold surface, the fog is referred to as 'sea fog'). One of the most significant differences between advection fog and radiation fog is that advection fog will often be found when there are moderate winds blowing, something that never happens with radiation fog. Indeed, wind is one of the necessary criteria for a sea fog to develop because the warm, moist air has to blow in over the cold sea. While the still conditions associated with radiation fog tend to give the familiar conditions you expect for fog over land, there is something very eerie about a situation when the wind may be blowing force 4 or 5, there are moderate seas running, and this is combined with greatly reduced visibility. It creates a very uncomfortable set of weather circumstances for yachts.

The physical processes involved in the formation of sea fog are similar to those found with radiation fog. The warm, moist air has to come into contact with a surface whose temperature is below the dew point of this nearly saturated air, so that when the air cools in contact with the colder surface, the water vapour condenses and the fog forms. The main difference between the formation of radiation fog and sea fog is in the nature of the cooling surface. The temperature of the sea surface varies only slightly through heating by the sun and through loss of heat because of radiation at night-time, and varies very little from day to day, or day to night. This means that the occurrence of sea fog tends not to depend either on the time of the day or the state of the sky and it doesn't need the clear skies that are a characteristic of the formation of radiation fog. Sea fog needs a warm, moist wind, so in northern waters it is generally associated with a south-westerly wind blowing in from the Atlantic. Advection fog can often persist for considerable periods, even days, until there is significant change in the conditions – which usually means a change in the direction of the wind.

Sea fog is virtually unknown in more southern waters such as the Mediterranean, and is much more a feature of temperate and high latitude areas where cold water currents exist. In these areas it generally occurs in the spring or early summer when the sea is still cold, and the air passing over it can be relatively warm and moist because it has either originated in lower latitudes or passed over warmer land masses, which start to heat up with the arrival of spring.

Fog in the forecast

By looking at topography and local conditions, you can better understand why the forecaster might have a problem in forecasting fog or mist. When extensive fog is expected, the forecaster can usually assess the conditions and include this in the forecast, and you can be fairly certain that this will be a sea fog. What he may not be so good at is forecasting local fogs, where radiation fog is usually the culprit. With a forecast of extensive fog you are left in little doubt about the situation, while with fog patches you may or may not be affected. In fog patches, the fog may envelop you just when you are engaged

'…The temperature of the sea surface varies very little from day to day.'

in some critical navigation manoeuvre, so the important thing here is to try to identify the type of fog being forecast so you have a better idea of where and how it might be expected, and plan a strategy accordingly.

When you wake up to fog in the morning or fog is forecast, what you really want to know is when it will clear, because this is what will affect your planning and strategy. The radiation fog you wake up with will hopefully clear by mid morning if the sun does its job. With advection fog, generally a change of wind direction is needed. With radiation fog you should be able to feel your way out of harbour with a degree of confidence that it will clear once you are outside. You are more likely to encounter advection fog when you are out at sea, and then you are faced with the challenge of getting back into harbour; so this is the fog that presents the real challenge. Once you have identified that it is sea fog surrounding you, the weather forecasts will give you the best idea of potential for clearance and help you decide on a strategy either to make a safe passage or hole up in an anchorage until the fog clears.

Drizzle

Visibility can also be restricted by drizzle out at sea. Drizzle tends to form in an occluded front, formed as the associated low pressure starts to weaken when the warm and cold fronts have come together. The winds are generally light in these fronts, and in drizzle the visibility could be down to perhaps just half a mile, but that should not pose navigation problems as long as you have electronic support. It is more the miserable conditions than the visibility that will hamper navigation. You can get the same visibility restrictions in thunderstorms and very heavy rain but these tend to be quite short-lived, although the rain can seriously affect your radar capability. You may struggle to pick up buoys and small craft on the radar during heavy rain and even larger ships could disappear for a time, but generally you will still be able to see the land features. One point to consider when using radar in rain is that wet sails can reduce the effectiveness of the radar signal so if your radar antenna in located halfway up the mast or on a pole at the stern, there may be restricted radar coverage ahead.

Try to keep out of the shipping lanes in fog.

Coping with fog

You face two problems in fog. One is seeing other vessels and avoiding collisions and the other is navigating safely to harbour. The main concern when navigating in fog is the increased risk of collision with other vessels in the vicinity. The COLREGs require that you operate at a 'safe' speed in fog, but they do not define what is safe. It could be argued that a safe speed is one where you don't have a collision. These days most ships maintain their full speed irrespective of the visibility, relying entirely on their radar to avoid collision. Hopefully your boat will show up on their radar, which is a good reason to have a radar reflector or a radar transponder fitted, and if you have an AIS fitted, then there is an even better chance you will be detected. Even if you are detected, there is no guarantee that the ship will take avoiding action because the navigator on the bridge will have his hands full under fog conditions and your small target may seem irrelevant, so one of my first actions in fog is to try to navigate in waters where the big ships do not or cannot venture.

Ships usually operate along quite clearly defined routes and these tend to be quite a distance offshore, so inshore waters are a safer option for yachts to operate in. Any waters with a depth of under around 15m (50ft) are also likely to be free of shipping, so this opens up the possibility of segregating yourself from the threat of shipping. As a general rule, shipping will pass at least 5 miles off a headland, but you cannot be entirely sure of this. In harbour channels marked by buoys, remember that these buoys are generally laid to mark the deep water shipping channels used by ships. You will often be able to navigate on what would be considered the 'wrong' side of the buoys, which puts you outside the main channel where you can still use the buoys for navigation, but you know the big ships pose no threat because they are on the other side – however, do check on the chart that the buoys are not laid close to the shallows. Some harbours even have dedicated channels for small craft to ensure this separation. If you can avoid the ships, you cut down the collision risk considerably, and all you have to do then is consider other boats that may be out there.

Safe speed

Taken to its logical conclusion, a 'safe' speed would be one where you do not have a collision; but in reality it is one where, when you sight another vessel, you have time to stop or alter course before a collision occurs. You might take this to mean that it is safe to stop within the range of the visibility, but this is not the case. Two vessels approaching one another in fog will meet somewhere in the middle of the range of visibility, so to ensure a safe, collision-free speed, you need to be able to stop within half the range of the visibility.

Working out the range of visibility in fog is not always easy and you will only get a good idea when you sight a fixed object such as a buoy. By using the GPS you can work out your distance from the buoy and assess the range of visibility. If you are leaving harbour in poor visibility, you should be able to get a range measurement as you leave. In either case, you have to remember that the range can change significantly over a short period of time, so any measurement you make may not be valid for long.

At the end of the day, you will have to estimate the range of visibility as you go along and any measurements you can make from a buoy or other fixed object will help you to build up the experience to do this. Then you need to know the stopping distance of your boat and this is something you can measure quite easily with GPS readings. On a sailboat you will not be sailing in radiation fog because there will be no wind, so your speed under power will depend on the stopping capability when you go into reverse – which is not always the strong point of sailboat auxiliary engines. In advection fog you may still be under sail but it is sensible to have your engine running ready for an emergency. A point to remember is that a sailboat coming out of the fog with white sails and a white hull will not be easily seen by another vessel because it merges into the fog background.

The range of visibility might be quite good but on a practical level it is only as good as when you actually see the other vessel, which could occur some way inside the range

Buoys can provide a good position check in fog but beware that other boats may be heading for them as well.

of visibility. As with night driving, running the boat on autopilot can relieve you of the pressure of steering the boat and give you more time for a lookout; but remember that other boats could be hidden behind the sails, so a lookout located in the bow might be a good idea if you have the sails up. Taking avoiding action by steering out of trouble rather than reversing is another option and you need to be familiar with the location of the 'standby' button on the autopilot so you can quickly disconnect it.

Sound signals

According to the COLREGs you are obliged to make sound signals to warn other craft of your presence. This regulation is largely ignored by both ships and boats and I cannot remember when I last heard a fog signal from another vessel at sea, even though it can be a great help for any small craft without radar that might be in your locality.

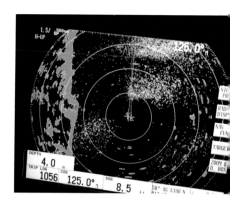

Rain squalls show up on radar and can affect the detection of small craft.

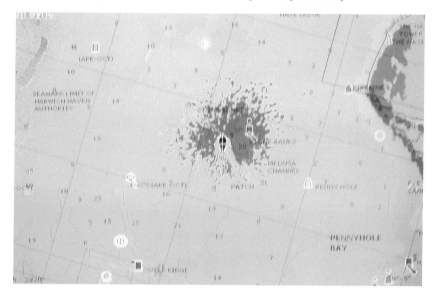

Sea clutter on the radar can hide small craft in the vicinity.

Using radar in fog

Radar can make a huge difference when you are navigating in fog, even though it will not offer 100 per cent certainty of detection. In theory it will simply give you a picture of all the vessels and navigation marks around you, as well as the land features; but imagine a situation where you are in a sea fog and the fog is matched to a fresh breeze that is generating a lively sea. The radar will also pick up those waves, with their returns being as strong as those from a small boat. You can reduce this sea clutter by adjusting the controls, but in so doing you also reduce the sensitivity of the radar in the area close around your boat, so there will be less chance of picking up returns from small boats.

There is no way to discriminate between sea clutter and small boat returns, so in practice you will not always know the boat is there until you actually see it. Radar reflectors and transponders will help detection but are not the complete answer. So even with radar, caution is needed and that vital visual lookout should not be relaxed, particularly in the approaches to harbours where there could be a few small angling boats at sea, even in fog.

' ...Radar can make a huge difference when you are navigating in fog.'

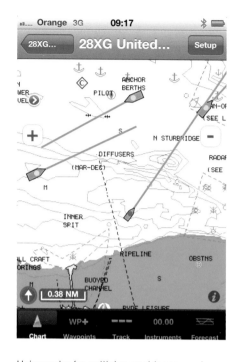

Using radar for collision avoidance requires some practice and skill in interpreting the radar picture. You will hopefully pick up the radar returns of other vessels and the first action here is to determine whether there is a risk of collision. You need to have the radar on a head-up presentation so that the targets are shown relative to your own vessel's heading. Now you use the same technique as you would with visual collision avoidance – check the relative bearing of the target and see if it is changing significantly. You do this by having the autopilot hold your boat on a steady course and then putting the bearing cursor onto the target. If the target stays on or close to the bearing cursor, there is a risk of collision and you need to take action. The COLREGs demand that you do this in good time before any close-quarters situation develops and that makes sense as it also gives the other vessel time to detect your actions long before you get close. This gets much more tricky when you have to deal with several targets at the same time – you might alter away from one and put yourself in the way of another.

If you have any doubts about what to do in a multi-vessel situation, slow down right to where you can just maintain steerage way and buy yourself some time to work it out. Remember also to check out what is happening astern of you, because if you are going slowly there might be other vessels overtaking you.

Some more sophisticated small boat radars have a MARPA capability where any vessel targets detected can show their course and speed vector. You select the target you wish to know about and the radar then shows its direction of travel with the length of the vector line relating to the speed. When you click on the target a box will show the Closest Point of Approach (CPA) and alarms can be set to warn you of approaching dangerous targets. For MARPA to work effectively, the radar needs your own course and speed through the water and not course and speed over the ground, and it is best to be running under autopilot control and on a steady heading.

Above left: AIS feeds onto smartphones and other devices can show headings of ships but there is a serious time lag.

Above right: A radar feed overlaying the electronic chart can help in identifying moving and fixed targets.

Surviving fog

In fog you need to maintain a high level of concentration at all times, and constantly looking into the nothingness of fog is not easy. It is very unlikely you will pick out another vessel at the maximum range of visibility unless you happen to be looking in the right direction at the right time. If you are unfortunate enough to have the combination of fog and darkness, perhaps this is the time to seek harbour or a safe anchorage until things clear, although the lights of another vessel will be more visible than the vessel itself. Remember always to put on your own navigation lights in fog, even in daylight.

Navigating in fog

As for navigating your boat in fog, the electronic chart becomes a vital tool and you follow the same techniques as in clear weather. It is helpful to set a course that will pass quite close to a buoy, so that when you sight it you will have that vital visual check on your position and also get an idea of what the visibility actually is. If you have to make a landfall in fog or any sort of poor visibility, make your approach at an angle to the shoreline. If you head straight in when you sight the shore, you will have a full 180° to turn to head away and you will have the dilemma of which way to turn. Approaching at an angle, there is a much shallower turn to make and there is only one obvious way to turn. With the electronic chart and/or the radar for navigation you are unlikely to have to use this technique, but it was one we used a lot before the advent of electronics and it demonstrates how you can find ways to make life in fog easier and safer.

There is no easy solution to navigating in fog and your workload can increase dramatically. Ideally you want one person concentrating on the radar alone, to watch the sequence of events developing (this is essential if your radar display is at the chart table below). It is best if your radar has the facility of a split screen, showing two radar ranges at the same time. You use, say, the 6-mile range to see the bigger picture of what is going on around you and a shorter, perhaps 3-mile range to decide on any collision avoidance manoeuvres. If only one range is available, the choice is likely to be between the 3- and 6-mile ranges, reducing the range even further when you are in harbour waters. With just a single screen display available, you should be able to have the radar superimposed onto the electronic chart display. This puts a lot of information onto one display and you will need to concentrate harder to pick out any small targets on the screen. However, such a display does have the advantage of being able to relate a radar target to a fixed buoy shown on the chart.

The real challenge in fog is when your boat is not fitted with radar and that applies to many sailboats. In this case, your only information about other vessels comes from your visual lookout. Again, have one crew member dedicated to this alone. It can be tough trying to concentrate on looking around the horizon when there is nothing to see, so change the lookout frequently to maintain vigilance.

Fog is best avoided on a cruise if you can and I would certainly hesitate to go to sea when there is a forecast of sea fog. I would probably hesitate just as much if it were radiation fog, unless the harbour entrance is straightforward and you know it is clear outside. Best wait for that fog to clear, and with the good phone communications now often available at sea it can help to phone ahead for information about the extent of the fog. With a radiation fog you can take the chance of heading out in the strong hope that out at sea it will be clear and you will find bright sunshine and glorious sailing. Plan ahead carefully if you choose to do this, both to check the navigation out from the harbour and for the movements of other vessels.

Fog brings a whole new dimension to navigating, one where intense concentration may be required; but it is one where modern electronic systems have helped to ease the navigation burden considerably.

9

Adventure cruising

A whole new focus

You might be very happy cruising from port to port, enjoying the time at sea and navigating your boat, but there is an alternative side to cruising. Adventure cruising moves on from the normal and allows skippers to visit places that are off the beaten track or perhaps challenge their navigation skills more than just the port-to-port voyage.

For the cruiser/racer it could involve fitting in some local regattas along the way and enjoying the sailing and social life; or it might involve getting up close and personal with the shoreline or with rocks, or moving out of your comfort zone and into a more challenging environment where the GPS has only limited application and you have to rely on more traditional forms of navigation. For some, such a cruise can allow you to get close to nature in a way that is not possible on land or into places that are only accessible from the sea.

You can visit remote islands and venture into the relative unknown. This is adventure cruising, which can bring a whole new focus to your voyages.

My introduction to adventure cruising was off the west coast of Scotland in a time when marinas were virtually unheard of in those remote island regions. When we wanted fresh water we went ashore in the tender and filled up containers from a stream. There was little in the way of pilot guides to help us and the scale of the charts meant you did not have too much faith in what they were showing inshore. We would feel our way into an anchorage, nudging closer inshore and peering intently at the echo sounder and over the bow into the clear water to see when it was shoaling and the right depth for anchoring. Seals would pop up their heads to see what this intruder into their world was up to. It taught me to be self-sufficient when cruising, to plan ahead as far as supplies were concerned, and there was enormous satisfaction at the end of a week in these challenging conditions where the rewards were silent anchorages and peace and quiet among the mountain scenery.

> ' …You can visit remote islands and venture into the relative unknown. '

Below left: Adventure cruising can bring you close to wildlife.

Below: There are many idyllic anchorages in remote locations.

One way to get a taste of adventure cruising is to switch off your electronics and try to undertake a cruise from port to port using only the traditional means of navigation. This can really keep you on your toes and not only is it good practice for if and when your electronics might fail but there is also enormous satisfaction in making it work. I was forced into this situation a couple of years ago when taking an 80-year-old converted Dutch fishing boat down the Adriatic and around the bottom of Italy using just traditional navigation because there was nothing else. Instead of looking at electronic displays I had to look out of the windows and pick up every clue about position and progress. It was exciting and extremely satisfying when we arrived. You think it is quite straightforward until the fog comes down and you lose the visibility. It does make you realise how things have changed; but that was how we navigated 50 years ago and the techniques still work today and are worth learning.

When I look back, most of my early boating was a form of adventure cruising and to a certain extent we have lost some of the fun and the challenge of those days. Yes, there was a higher risk factor to contend with, but that taught you seamanship and skills that can be hard to find today. Adventure cruising is not for everyone and you must decide what level of risk and excitement you want from your cruising. Certainly you will need to build up your level of experience gradually and even though we have become rather risk averse with all the safety warnings and cosseting from the authorities, there are still plenty of challenges out there for those who want to seek them out.

In Northern Europe there is still scope for adventure cruising, with areas like the west coast of Scotland, the Scilly Isles and much of the coast of France offering good possibilities to get away from the crowds and find a secluded anchorage for the night. The west coast of Ireland could be a Mecca for the adventure cruising enthusiast, and here there is hardly a marina in sight. You can find safe and secure harbours that have been established mainly for the fishing fleets, but much of this exposed coastline is still wild and untamed. In the Mediterranean it is much harder to get off the beaten track with many of the potential anchorages now occupied by marinas, and what might look like a secluded bay on the

Adventure cruising can open many possibilities.

The Skye Bridge is the gateway to a world of remote islands and wonderful scenery.

chart, suitable for an overnight anchorage, might already be full of yachts when you arrive. There are still places further east where you can find remote islands and coastlines, such as among the Greek islands and on the east coast of the Adriatic, but development seems to be spreading fast. One bay on the island of Capri that I visited recently looked very promising on the chart but on arrival it was full of mooring buoys and superyachts, and the first visitor was the harbour master, wanting payment for staying there.

Above left: A remote small harbour in the Mediterranean.

Above right: Stunning rock formations in the Mediterranean.

Adventure cruising in a sailboat

The average sailboat may not be the best type of vessel for exploring a coastline and rocks close inshore because of its keel shape, which means you may have a draft of perhaps 2 metres (6 ft). With the shape of the hull of the average yacht you cannot consider drying out over a low tide and that will restrict your access to many smaller and more remote harbours. However, this can be the time when you need a capable tender so that you find your suitable anchorage and then use the tender for further exploration. A small RIB tender or inflatable powered by an outboard motor can give you access to many exciting and remote places that others cannot reach.

Catamarans can be great for adventure cruising because of their shallow draft.

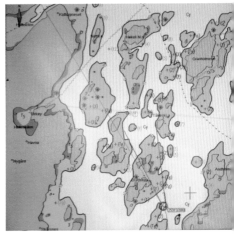

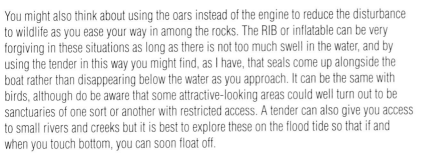

You might also think about using the oars instead of the engine to reduce the disturbance to wildlife as you ease your way in among the rocks. The RIB or inflatable can be very forgiving in these situations as long as there is not too much swell in the water, and by using the tender in this way you might find, as I have, that seals come up alongside the boat rather than disappearing below the water as you approach. It can be the same with birds, although do be aware that some attractive-looking areas could well turn out to be sanctuaries of one sort or another with restricted access. A tender can also give you access to small rivers and creeks but it is best to explore these on the flood tide so that if and when you touch bottom, you can soon float off.

If you have a bilge keel yacht or one with a lifting keel or centreboard that will allow you to take the bottom over a low tide, you could have access to many small ports and harbours around the coast. Many of the harbours on the British coastline were developed when sea transport was the only viable means of moving heavy cargoes around the coast. Roads and railways had not been developed to any significant extent, so nearly every coastal village and town had a harbour of sorts. Some of these even date back to Roman times and many were developed to export local minerals and farm produce. If you are interested in industrial archaeology, getting access to these small harbours could be the focus of a cruise. Almost without exception you will need a yacht that will take the ground to get access to these harbours, but there is always the alternative of anchoring off and coming in by tender. There will often be a pub ashore to welcome you, and perhaps a village store.

One point to remember when entering these drying harbours, even in remote areas, is that most of the good moorings in the harbour will probably be occupied by local boats. You may be able to pick up one of their moorings if you check first with the harbour master or the boatmen, but if you plan to anchor, then the only spots available are likely to be in one of the more exposed areas of the harbour, which could be fine in settled weather conditions. Many of these harbours have a cat's cradle of anchor and mooring lines over the seabed, so finding a clear anchorage can be difficult – but the harbours can be fascinating places to visit so are worth the effort.

Another option in a drying harbour can be to tie up alongside the quay and dry out there. A lot of these small harbours still retain a quay where the cargoes were handled, and this might be available as a temporary berth overnight.

Above left: Small harbours can be exciting destinations but you have to be prepared to be more self-sufficient.

Above right: Islands make great destinations for exploring.

Bilge keel yachts are designed to dry out at moorings if necessary.

This fin and bulb keel is not a good solution if you want the yacht to dry out at a mooring.

Prepare to be flexible

When you are adventure cruising you need to be a lot more flexible in your planning because the weather is likely to have a much more significant impact on what you can and cannot do. You will be called upon to make more judgement calls about what is feasible to achieve on a day's cruise and a night in harbour or at anchor. You need to have the confidence that comes from experience to achieve this and you need back-up plans to enable you to cope with short-term changes. The reward for this is the enormous pleasure to be found from adventure cruising, which can add a whole new dimension to your boating. This is something to try when the marinas and crowded harbours of regular summer cruising may pall. When you go boating off the beaten track in this way, you will need more planning and more attention to detail – but at the end of the day, successful adventure cruising is all about having confidence in your abilities and those of your boat.

This can often work for a temporary overnight berth in settled conditions – the local boats don't do this because there can be a considerable surge when there is a strong wind, and they are there on a permanent basis with their own moorings. You will need to work out the mooring ropes and fenders carefully and possibly have a rope or two onto the quay from the mast that will hold the boat upright as it dries out. Many of the quay walls in these small harbours are built of rough stone, so good fendering is essential; and you may not get the most peaceful night's sleep if the boat dries out or floats again in the middle of the night. If you do dry out in this way, however, it can be a good opportunity to check out the rudder and propeller without having the cost of a lift-out.

When you are exploring in this way you will need to keep a careful watch on the weather. An anchorage or a berth in a small harbour that looked secure when you came in may change its character considerably if the wind freshens from another direction. It is not just the wind that can affect things but also the swell, and what might look like a low gentle swell when you are out in the open seas can turn much nastier when it hits the shallows. What might look like an easy harbour entrance in fine conditions can become a mass of white water when a swell comes in or even when the tide turns. But then this is what adventure cruising is all about – making your own assessment of the conditions, and looking ahead and planning what you do and where you go according to the prevailing conditions. You move a bit nearer the edge but you will build up a level of self-confidence in your cruising abilities and get to places and have experiences that the conventional cruise cannot match.

Watching the sunset with a glass in your hand

Finding a quiet anchorage for the night can be one of the joys of cruising. There is nothing quite like finding a secluded cove, dropping the anchor, and watching the sunset with a glass in your hand. Unfortunately, secluded coves are becoming harder to find and you do need care to ensure you get a quiet night's sleep. What might look like a nice sheltered cove when you anchor could turn out to be quite lively by the morning if the wind has changed and the cove is more exposed. So the weather forecast will be your guide for finding the required degree of shelter, perhaps over a period of 12 hours while you are there.

Anchorage

Finding a sheltered anchorage for the night is the first challenge and if you want a peaceful night you need to find a cove where there will be no sea or swell intruding. This is not as easy as it sounds, and the first step is to look at the weather. A cove that is sheltered in the evening can be very uncomfortable in the morning if the wind has swung round to leave you exposed. Weather forecasts are normally reliable enough to indicate whether there might be any threat of this. You need extra care if the wind is freshening because this can generate a swell as well as more lively seas. Another problem is when you look at the chart and indentify what looks like a great sheltered cove, only to arrive to find it is untenable with a rolling swell coming in that could make that night at anchor very uncomfortable. This is because when a swell rounds a headland it tends to be refracted around the headland and directed into the bay behind. It is a simple law of physics that can make a bay that is sheltered from the west wind still have a swell coming in from the south or south-west. So you need to choose your anchorage with care, having regard to the weather forecast and what the wind has been for the past 24 hours. There are good pilot guides that indicate problems of this nature in potential anchorages, so read up about the places you plan to visit and think about what the wind and the tides will be doing.

Left: Small harbours can be worth visiting but space may be limited.

Right: A quiet mooring in the Scottish Highlands.

Finding an anchorage

It can appear to be a nice sheltered bay on the chart and the perfect place to anchor for lunch, but take a very close look before you pick your spot to anchor. It can help a lot to know what the seabed consists of before you drop the hook, because sand and shingle make a good holding ground while in mud the hold can be much more tenuous. A rocky bottom is not good news because there may not be much for the anchor to grip on and if it does, it might prove very difficult to free it from the position where it is locked in under a rock. Using an anchor buoy attached to the crown of the anchor can help to free an anchor lodged in this way.

The paper chart will generally show you what the seabed consists of, but this is not always the case with electronic charts. The pilot book may give some indication but otherwise you may have to try to get clues from looking at the shore. If you see a sandy beach, the chances are this will extend out into the bay, although some sandy beaches turn to rock as the water gets deeper. Rocks on the shore may extend out into the bay, but equally they can give way to a sandy bottom. Of course, in clear water you simply have to look overboard to see what is on the bottom. Mud on the bottom is usually found in

rivers and estuaries and hard clay might exist where there is a strong scouring by the current.

Other hazards to watch out for are any submarine cables shown on the chart and of course any mooring buoys, where the actual moorings can extend some way out from the buoy itself. Finally there may be lobster pots in the nice secluded bay and their presence could indicate the rocky bottom favoured by lobsters and crabs.

It is not always easy to get away from the crowd in remote areas these days.

X marks the spot

You can mark your chosen anchorage spot on the chart with a cross – but then you have to find that spot. Obviously you can come in on the GPS, taking care that your route avoids any off-lying rocks or shoals; but if you do this, back up the GPS positioning with checks on the echo sounder. Rather than aim for a particular spot, it is often better to work your way slowly in with the echo sounder running and wait to anchor until the sounder shows a particular chosen depth, bearing in mind the rise and fall of the tide when selecting the depth. This way you can get in as close to the shore as is comfortable and perhaps get more shelter under a headland. Finding a good anchorage for the night is a skill that develops with experience, and what you think is shelter does not always turn out that way. I had a wild night at anchor off the west coast of Scotland when what I thought was a very sheltered cove was made untenable by the wild squalls that swept down off the lee side of the mountains.

Chart information

When you are going in among the rocks or close to the coastline, be aware that the information on the chart may not be as reliable as you might like. From the chart maker's point of view there is not a lot of point in spending time and effort surveying these areas where normally boats would not think about entering, so often you will need to feel your way in slowly. You have to rely heavily on visual navigation for this and of course there is no problem in seeing what is above the water. It is what lies below that will concern you more and here you use a combination of the echo sounder and looking over the bow. Fortunately, the water among rocks is usually quite clear so seeing what lies below should not be a problem – but remember that looking at rocks through water can often give a distorted view. Waves will also break on rocks that are close to the surface, giving an early indication of dangers.

Coming into an anchorage for a peaceful night away from the crowds.

Beach landing

A tender can allow you to land on remote beaches where there is a thrill about leaving footsteps on virgin sand. There are many beaches and coves that are only accessible from the sea and this can be a great way to get privacy away from the summer crowds. Some care is needed for beach landings because while the landing is relatively easy, getting off again may present difficulties. In the Mediterranean, where there is little or no tide, beach landings are relatively easy, but where there is a rise and fall of the tide more care is needed. Your tender is probably light enough to be carried up the beach and then launched again when you head back. If there are waves breaking on the beach, you need extra care when landing because it is very easy for the boat to get picked up and capsized. The problem is that,

You do need a settled weather forecast before you attempt landing on a beach.

when coming in from seaward, it is not always easy to see just how big the surf is on the beach, so wait just outside the surf line for a while to get a better picture of the conditions. On a gently shelving beach there will be several lines of breakers and in reasonable conditions you should be able to negotiate these quite easily as long as you keep up speed on the boat. On a steep-to beach the waves will break in one big dump that could take you along with it and literally dump you on the beach. As long as you are prepared to get wet when landing and getting off, there should not be a major problem as long as the conditions are moderate.

Some brave souls think about putting their yacht onto the beach over a tide, but for this you need a very sheltered beach and a yacht that will dry out safely, such as a bilge keeler. It is best to put out an anchor over the stern as you come into the beach, which will serve to keep the yacht in position as the tide rises again and also help to pull the yacht off if that is necessary.

Finding a peaceful anchorage amongst the rocks.

Anchor lines

If you are a marina cruiser, you are only likely to use your anchor in an emergency situation and it will not be high on your list of priorities. However, if you plan to anchor as part of your cruising itinerary you need to consider your anchor and its fittings in more detail. Assuming that you have an adequate size of anchor for your boat, your focus should be on the anchor line.

On yachts where weight can be important for performance, you might have a rope anchor line to save weight. A rope line is fine if the anchor is only used for a temporary anchorage, say over lunch, but for overnight anchoring something more substantial is required. Chain is the traditional material for the anchor line – the extra weight of the chain makes the anchor hold better, and chain is also resistant to chafe, while a rope line is susceptible to chafe from stones, rocks or even gravel on the seabed. There is also the risk of chafe at the point where a rope leaves the boat, such as in a fairlead, so again a chain is the safe option – you will sleep more happily at night if you have chain connecting you to the anchor.

You can also use a combination of rope and chain, with a few metres of chain at the anchor end of the line to add weight and reduce chafe. There are capstans designed to handle this combination.

When anchoring, always put out a minimum anchor line of four times the depth of the water and allow for a rise in tide when you do the sums. As for the size of anchor, it should weigh in kilos about the same number as the length of the boat in metres, with a bit extra. Always have some means to secure the anchor in its bow fairlead or pipe when at sea so it can't come adrift through the constant movement of the boat, and when at anchor don't rely just on the capstan brake to hold the chain or rope. Finally, make sure that the inboard end of the anchor line is made fast to a secure point in the boat. There is nothing more embarrassing at sea than letting go the anchor and seeing the tail end disappearing overboard because you forgot to secure it. For serious adventure cruising you might want to consider carrying a spare anchor and line on board.

Top Tip

Cruising in winter

Cruising in the winter can be another form of adventure cruising. There is the pleasure of empty seas and easy access to ports and marinas – but more preparation is needed. You probably won't undertake this without heating in the yacht, but you will also need to consider your clothing very carefully so you can keep warm and dry. A series of layers is better than one thick suit, and good gloves, head covering and boots are essential. In the winter you should consider wearing lifejackets and making lifelines compulsory, and at all times be very conscious of the debilitating effects of long-term exposure to cold and wet. The rewards of winter cruising can be some spectacular scenery and the joys of an empty ocean.

10

Fuel management
and economy

Fuel considerations

Even though you are a sailboat owner, fuel still plays a vital role when cruising. The engine and its ability to keep you going – when the wind drops, or things go wrong, or you simply need to meet a schedule – can bring peace of mind and offer possibilities to cope with any emergency. It makes sense to have enough fuel on board to complete the planned passage if you need to switch to motor, but there is much more to consider than that. You may be concerned about operating economically to minimise fuel consumption; you may be able to use the fuel to help trim the boat; and these days there could be concerns about 'green issues' and emissions. Also, the fuel can be used to generate the electricity that seems so vital to operating a sailboat these days.

One of the main problems with fuel consumption is that on most sailboats you don't know how much of it you are using. At least, you know how much there is on board when the fuel tanks are filled up, because the builder's handbook tells you the capacity of the tanks – but do you have any idea how much fuel is going through the engines at any one time, and do you know how much fuel it might take to complete a passage?

Of course, you can work it out afterwards by checking what is left in the tanks – but to be meaningful you really want to know what the engines are burning as you go along. You can look at the engine manufacturer's charts, which will show the theoretical amount of fuel the engines are burning at any given rpm. With modern diesels there is a way to find out what the real time fuel consumption is using the computer controls that operate on most engines today. Even on small sailboat engines you should be able to get a readout on the engine monitoring display of how many litres per hour the engine is burning. That is a useful figure and you can immediately see how the fuel consumption of the engine rises and falls when you open or close the throttle to adjust the speed.

Relating consumption to speed

However, these figures only tell you half the story because they do not relate to the speed of the boat and therefore the distance travelled. What you really want to know is how many litres per mile are being used (or how many miles per litre you are doing). A fuel consumption meter in your car tells you how many miles you are getting to a litre of fuel, but to get this figure on a boat you have to take the litres per hour figure and then factor in how many miles you have covered in that hour (see panel). It is a cumbersome way of reaching the figure but the problem is that the engine computer does not normally have a GPS input, which would enable the computer to work out the speed and from that the litres per mile figure.

A small sail drive unit is a great solution for smaller sailboats.

Litres per mile

Assuming your boat has a modern electronic engine display that shows the fuel consumption in litres per hour, you can convert this to the much more useful litres per mile figure. You simply divide the litres per hour figure by your speed in knots and you have litres per mile. However, do remember that the main speed readout on board will come from the GPS, which gives the figure for speed over ground and not through water, so you may need to add or subtract a knot or two to allow for the tide influence.

It is a good idea to spend some time on a calm day taking fuel consumption figures throughout the speed range of the boat so you can draw up a graph of fuel consumption per mile. This will

be a valuable tool when doing your passage planning, and you simply multiply the litres per mile figure by the length of the passage to find out how much fuel you will need when running at that particular speed. Add on a reserve amount, perhaps 20 per cent, plus an allowance to get you to an alternative port at a greater distance than your chosen port. Finally, allow for the amount of fuel in the tank that will not be accessible and you have the minimum fuel quality you need to complete the passage under motor.

Do bear in mind that fuel consumption is likely to increase if you have a head wind on the passage. You may be able to save fuel if you keep the sails up, so that effectively you are motor sailing.

The engine compartment on a sailboat may not always allow easy accessibility.

The fuel filter should be easy to access for cleaning.

Assessing the fuel situation

So with these figures available, and knowing how many miles you are planning to travel on your cruise, you can calculate how much fuel you will need. That is the easy part; the complications set in when you try to check the amount of fuel you have on board and what level of reserve fuel you should carry. The manual will tell you how much the fuel tanks hold, but does it tell you how much of that fuel is useable? Any water or dirt in the fuel settles out on the bottom of the tank and it is not good practice to draw this into the engine so, in almost all fuel tanks, the suction pipe connecting the tank to the engine is above the bottom of the tank. This means that as much as 10 per cent of the fuel in the tank is not available for use – which is fine if you know about it, but the next question is about the accuracy of fuel gauges. It is important that you know firstly how accurate your gauge is and secondly if the amount indicated does or does not include the section of unusable fuel at the bottom of the tank. Gauges that simply show ¼, ½, ¾ and full do not give you the level of accuracy you require, and without doubt the best type is the sight gauge, a clear vertical tube attached to the tank where the level in the tube matches that inside the tank. It is simple, reasonably accurate, there is nothing to go wrong, and it even works with a power failure; the only disadvantage is that you have to go into the engine or tank compartment to read it. You can calibrate the sight gauge by marking your reserve level on the tube, then adding fuel at the rate of, say, 20 litres at a time and making incremental marks. Fuel tanks are not always evenly shaped and it is common to find them with a narrower cross-section at the bottom than at the top to fit into the shape of the hull.

Diesel bug

'Diesel bug' is an organism that can grow and multiply in diesel fuel and will eventually lead to clogging of fuel lines and filters and generally prevent the engine operating effectively. The build-up tends to be slow and steady, so if you clean your fuel filters frequently you should become aware of diesel bug before it gets serious, because of the 'gunge' you find there. Once in the fuel system it is very hard to get rid of. There are various 'disinfectants' that are claimed to cure the problem, but it is much better to prevent it altogether and the best safeguard is to always get your fuel from a reliable source.

EU legislation dictates that fuel supplied for boats that operate on inland waterways and on recreational craft 'when not at sea' must in future operate on sulphur-free diesel fuel. Just what qualifies as 'sulphur-free' is not quite clear at the time of writing, but the sulphur content in fuel helps to reduce the diesel bug problem so it may become more rife when sulphur-free fuel is introduced. At present, sea-going boats are exempt; but how long that will last is an open question. Another possibility in the future is the use of bio-diesel, also thought to be more prone to the diesel bug. This whole question of safe fuel is a thorny one for boaters and again the best solution I can offer is to get your fuel from a reliable source and to check your filters at regular intervals.

Going green

Fuel regulations are being introduced in the name of greener boating and to reduce carbon emissions. At every boat show these days you find even sailboats coming onto the market claiming to have green credentials. Of course, with a sailboat the best way to go green is to rely solely on wind propulsion; but there are sailboats now with electric propulsion and there are questions about just how green these are.

Hybrid systems
Much of the current focus of so-called green yachts is on hybrid systems, so let's have a look at those first. In many hybrid systems there is a combined generator and electric motor included in the drive train between the engine and the propeller. This generates electrical power when the diesel engine is running and this is fed to a large bank of batteries, where it is stored until needed. The battery bank then supplies electrical power back to the generator/motor when it is needed for propulsion, so the diesel engine can be switched off and you have wonderful silent propulsion with no emissions.

This sounds like the ultimate emission-free propulsion system – but think again. You have used the diesel engine to generate the electrical power that is stored in the batteries and then used to power the motor, so emissions have been generated in order to provide that electrical power. In fact, by using a hybrid system you are actually producing more emissions than you would if a straight diesel drive were used. This is because every time you use diesel fuel to generate electricity, send it to the batteries, and then take the power from the batteries to feed an electric motor, there are considerable losses – perhaps around 10 per cent with every step on the journey. That can amount to around 40 per cent of efficiency loss by the time the electrical power reaches the propeller, so in fact you are far less green when using a hybrid system.

A heavy duty battery charger is an essential piece of equipment these days.

Batteries need to be accessible for checking fixings and connections.

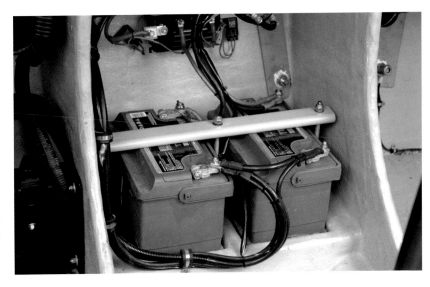

> ‘ *…with boats there is no fuel or emission saving with a hybrid system.* ’

Of course, the yacht salesman will tell you that you can enter harbour with no emissions if you use electric propulsion, but emissions have to be produced somewhere and they are just as harmful out at sea. You might think you are doing your bit by charging the batteries up from shore power, but again that electrical power has to be generated somewhere. So think carefully about using hybrid systems if you want a clean green conscience. Sure, you will get quiet propulsion when you want peace and quiet and electric power can make harbour manoeuvring a more precise operation; but with a hybrid system adding around 10 per cent to the overall cost of the boat, you are paying a lot and achieving very little. Car manufacturers are making emission savings from hybrid systems because they can recover energy from braking or when going downhill and this 'free' energy is fed back into the system. You hope your boat will never ever be going downhill and any braking requires engine power, so with boats there is no fuel or emission saving with a hybrid system.

There is also the additional weight of the hybrid system from the motors, batteries and control system. This can be significant and will reduce performance and once again add to the emissions rather than reduce them, because of the extra power needed to compensate for the additional weight.

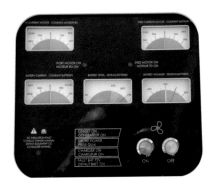

The monitoring panel on a hybrid powered yacht that shows the battery state and power consumption.

A better solution is a form of hybrid system where a diesel-powered generator produces electricity. The propeller is driven only by the electric motor, with no direct connection to the diesel, and the power from the generator is sent directly to the propulsion motors, or to the batteries, or split between them. Because the generator is running at a constant economical speed it should be more efficient than diesel propulsion engines, and will also give you an efficient means of battery charging in harbour or when at anchor. Such a system could work well on a catamaran, where a single generator would power an electric propulsion motor in each hull.

The larger bank of batteries you need with any hybrid system can be a bonus on a sailboat and should be adequate to meet the electric demands even on an overnight passage. A larger bank of batteries should be stowed low down in the hull, where it will contribute to the ballast requirements; but being low means that if water gets inside the hull, the batteries will be the first thing to go, just when you might need their power for the radio.

Most modern sailboats rely heavily on electrical power to provide onboard services and this can place heavy demands on the batteries. Essential to modern sailboats are the electronic navigation systems, the autopilot, the navigation lights, the radio, the fridge, and probably a means to charge your laptop, iPad and smartphone. Many toilet and fresh-water systems also use electrical power, albeit only intermittently. These are in addition to always having enough power for engine starting, although a separate battery dedicated to the engine requirements is usually installed so it is not drained by domestic use. Many modern diesel engines are computer controlled and will not operate without electrical power being available. The electrical demands can be considerable, so the batteries need to be managed carefully when you are under sail.

A wind charger and solar panels give a belt and braces approach to battery charging.

Working out the power consumption of your yacht is not too difficult. Each piece of equipment is marked with a power rating indicating the number of amps it consumes when running. Adding these together gives you the total power consumption at any time. To work out the drain on the battery you need to know the amount of power generated by any auxiliary systems, such as solar panels, plus the generator charging rate on the engine. This is what is going into the battery, and if you subtract this figure from the consumption figure you will have the actual drain on the battery – although it could be positive if the charge exceeds consumption. The battery bank will be rated at so many amp/hours, so if you divide the amp/hour figure by the consumption figure you will have the number of hours the battery will last, a valuable figure on an overnight passage.

'…Wind generators generate more power than solar panels.'

Obviously the batteries are being charged when the engine is running, but many cruising yachtsmen use supplementary systems. Solar power feeds a small amount of charge into the batteries during daylight hours and is a good source of battery charging when the yacht is not in use. Finding somewhere to fit solar panels can be a challenge and the logical place if you have a wheelhouse or cuddy is on the roof of that. The coachroof top is not a good idea because the surface of the panels is slippery when wet. Some yachts use a solar array mounted on a panel over the transom.

Wind generators are another solution and generate more power than solar panels, probably enough to power most of the yacht's essential requirements. Wind generators are not pretty, they slow the boat down a bit, and they have to be mounted high, out of harm's way – but they will supply power both day and night as long as the wind is blowing, so can keep the batteries charged up on a night passage. Water generators are another option. These are towed behind the yacht or mounted on the transom and the propeller of the system turns to generate electricity. Again, they slow down the yacht slightly; also, you need to remember to take the towed variety in when entering harbour and, unlike other systems, they will not supply power in harbour. The fourth option, of course, is to run the engine – a very inefficient way to generate power, but it works in an emergency.

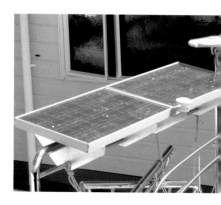

Solar panels provide a steady charge for the battery during the day but will not help at night when consumption usually goes up.

Above, left to right: Various locations for wind chargers on sailboats.

Some builders and designers are also focusing on reducing power demands on board by using anti-UV glass and LED lighting, which is more economical; and the electronics may have a standby mode to reduce consumption when not actually being used. Going green takes many forms.

Alternative fuels

There are also alternative fuels to consider. If you look at the car market, you will see the possibilities for cleaner fuels for sailboats in the future – bio-diesel, methanol, hydrogen, LPG and LNG. Some of these, such as bio-diesel, LPG and LNG, can work with slightly modified diesel engines, while methanol and hydrogen are probably best used in conjunction with fuel cells to generate electricity. There are vessels out there running on all these fuels, but they tend to be river and inland waterway vessels that operate close to their fuel source. For general use on sea-going yachts they are still a long way off in most cases. LPG and LNG are probably the most advanced and there are commercial vessels up to 100 metres (330 ft) long operating with gas as a fuel, but the availability of this fuel is the crucial factor and yacht-refuelling stations are a long way behind in this respect.

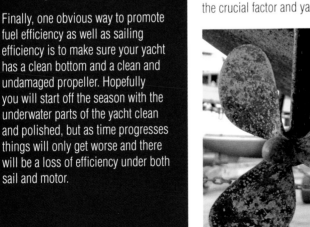

Above: There will be considerable drag from a non-feathering propeller.

Left: It is essential to keep the propeller clean for maximum efficiency.

11
Comfort on board

A home from home

Sitting alongside in the marina on a modern sailboat, you have all the luxury and facilities of modern life. It is amazing what today's designers can fit into the confined space within a hull and in most cases you can live on board in considerable luxury with most of the facilities you enjoy at home. There was a time when most boats were sold in a pretty basic form as far as the interior goes and it was up to the owner to tailor the interior to his requirements; but modern interiors are fully fitted out and, apart from some designated extras that normally have to be specified when ordering the boat from new, there is very little you can do to change things. The boat comes complete, and my worry is that sometimes the requirements for use in harbour take priority over the requirements for use at sea.

In harbour the boat is static, so everything, including the crew, stays in place. Out at sea the boat is moving most of the time – most probably heeling over under the influence of the sails – so things need to stay in place at quite steep angles. It is unlikely that a sailboat will heel over more than 15° under the influence of the wind, because any more and you will not be sailing efficiently – there can be rolls to a steeper angle, but it is better to reduce sail than go much beyond this angle on a cruising yacht. The yacht will also be rolling and pitching a bit in the waves, and even in light conditions there is always the risk that the wash of a passing boat or ship will start the boat moving.

Above left: Yachts can get crowded in port.

Above right: When the yacht is moving at sea you need secure accommodation to improve crew comfort.

Below: There is a steep climb up to the cockpit in this yacht.

This means that everything has to be secured in place – including the crew – and there need to be facilities for the crew to move about the boat in safety. A good designer will take all this into account, both inside and out, and the yacht will be as comfortable and secure as possible. Discomfort when you are cruising means you are likely to want to get into the calmer waters of harbour as quickly as possible and will not enjoy the scenic aspects of the cruise.

It is not too difficult to stow away all loose items before you leave harbour and that should be a standard part of your checklist. It is a question not only of putting stuff in drawers and lockers, but also making sure it can't rattle around inside. There is nothing more irritating than having rattles and knocks at sea, so ensuring everything is securely stowed should be a priority – bubble wrap can be very useful to stuff in drawers and lockers to hold the contents secure, and you want to be sure that both drawers and doors are secured. There are some things you will want to have out at sea, such as drinks and perhaps galley equipment if you plan to serve food. Cup holders are now fitted to many boats at the helm and these do a good job of holding things in place; and cup holders in the galley can help when pouring drinks. In general, however, there are few dedicated stowages like this available where you can put equipment you want to use at sea and this might be a modification you will want to carry out.

The galley

Using the galley at sea should be feasible and there is something very comforting about having hot drinks available when you are cruising. It is a sign that things are normal and under control if you can do this. However, I see so many boats where there is just a flat hob in the galley with no means of securing anything in place. Some of the more enterprising builders fit an adjustable fiddle rail on the hob and this is something you can probably add yourself if your boat is not already fitted. Fiddles not only allow you to use the stove for cooking at sea but also make a useful stowage for pots and pans when not in use. The alternative is to have a swinging cooker but these have largely gone out of fashion because the flexible connection for the electricity or gas can be vulnerable. For hot drinks, an electric kettle can be a great and relatively safe way to heat water, provided there is adequate battery power or mains available, and this can be secured in the fiddles while it is heating up.

However, at some stage you have to pour the hot water into mugs, possibly those insulated mugs that builders use. This requires two hands, so you have nothing left to hold on with, and this is where the cup holders can be useful. An alternative solution for this dilemma is the special non-skid plastic netting or sheeting that you place on a flat surface. This wonderful material should be on every surface on the boat that you use at sea and my experience is that it will hold things in place even when the boat is rolling up to 20°.

This canvas cuddy can provide weather protection at the helm.

Below left: The spacious accommodation that is found in the deck saloon of a catamaran.

Below right: A compact galley installation on a small cruising yacht.

It can make eating at a table much more comfortable because your plate will not go sliding away from you, but do use mugs for drinks because a cup is not very stable with its small base. Similarly it tends to be easier to eat from a bowl rather than a plate. Having this non-skid material on the work surfaces in the galley can make hot food preparation quite feasible even in quite lively sea conditions, which can be a boon for the blue water sailor who may have to provide food and drink for periods running into days rather than hours.

Handholds

It used to be standard to have a raised edge to tables, worktops and shelves on boats to stop things sliding off when the boat was rolling, but this is less common now, which is a pity because they serve the double function of stopping things sliding off and providing a handhold of sorts when you are moving about the boat. Personal security is important at sea and on some boats it can be a long way between handholds when you want to move, say, from the forward cabin to the cockpit door. Fittings on the furniture can help, as can an overhead handrail on the deckhead. You might need to consult the builders before fitting something like this because it will be useless unless it is secured to strong points on the boat. You might put a great deal of weight onto a handhold or handrail when you are moving about at sea so it needs to be strong and well secured.

As the saloons on yachts have become deeper and deeper to accommodate full headroom, so the ladders or steps up to the cockpit have become longer. You need handholds here both to climb the steps securely and possibly to hold on to while opening the doors.

It is not only security in the saloon you need to consider – at some stage on a voyage people will need to use the toilet, so you need handholds to go down below in safety and also in the toilet compartment. It would be nice to see builders and designers appreciating these difficulties but in some cases you feel that going to sea on a boat is a long way from their thoughts!

Above left: A comprehensive galley on a serious cruising yacht.

Above right: A fold-out small galley and a large sophisticated installation.

Below: Shelf edges and dedicated handholds are useful for crew security but they need to be strong.

Above left: It can be quite a climb from the cabin to the cockpit on some modern yachts

Above right: A vee berth like this works well in harbour but you could roll around at sea.

Below: Security is needed in the toilet compartment when heeled over at sea.

It is the same with sleeping arrangements, if you plan to make an overnight passage. There was a time when you had single bunks fitted with leeboards to keep you in place when you were sleeping. These days the best on offer is to wedge yourself in with a couple of pillows or cushions and hope you stay in place. On an overnight passage you may want to choose the lee bunks for sleeping because they are more secure, while saloon settees on the lee side can make a great place for a catnap and there will be less motion amidships if the yacht is pitching. Sleeping bags make a convenient form of bedding when you are at sea and are easily stowed and made ready for use, although they are not always the easiest things to get in and out of.

Temperature control and power supply

Sailboat interiors can get quite damp at sea with people coming below in wet oilskins and possibly wet sails being stowed forward. Ventilation is important to help keep the damp at bay and fresh air is a wonderful help for those suffering from seasickness, but it is not easy to achieve in lively conditions when there might be considerable spray flying around outside and you can't keep hatches or ports open. A heater can do a lot to keep dampness at bay but most heaters need an electric supply to power their fans as well as the basic fuel for heating and running those fans can deplete your battery reserves. The ones using diesel as a fuel will deplete your engine fuel supplies and those using gas, your cooking fuel supplies. Keeping warm and dry is the challenge in northern waters but in the Mediterranean you might want air-conditioning instead to keep things cool. You are not likely to use air-conditioning at sea even when it is hot but in harbour it can be a boon and you will usually have the shore power available to run it when you are in the marina. The blue water sailor will use wind chutes and other devices to funnel air down below when it is hot rather than add the complication and weight of an air-conditioning plant.

Refrigeration is now common on many sailboats and this can also add to the drain on the battery when the engine is not running. A fridge allows you to keep food for several days

Left: A saloon is great in harbour and these non-slip mats and table edging will help secure things at sea.

Below left and centre: Ventilation through skylights and opening portholes can help in warm weather.

Below: A dedicated chart table can be a great place to work on your computer.

and if you are on day cruises then it should still stay cool even when the fridge is switched off, as long as the door is not opened. You switch it on when the engine is running and when plugged in in harbour and by doing this you should be able to maintain the food and drink inside in cool condition. If you restrict the use of chargers for laptops, phones and iPads to the same regime, you should be able to have them operational at sea. For charging this equipment you may need an inverter that converts the 12- or 24-volt supply from the batteries into mains voltage; inverters also work well for low-demand power requirements.

Car-type chargers working on the low voltage can be an option. For items such as fan heaters, electric kettles and vacuum cleaners, the power requirements are a lot higher and these may only be used in harbour when you have a mains supply available. For water heating at sea, a low-voltage electric kettle can do the job but they do create quite a heavy drain on the battery. Wind and water chargers can be used at sea to help keep the batteries topped up and solar power can add a small contribution. You do need to manage your electric power supplies quite carefully at sea or when at anchor and a large bank of domestic batteries can help to spread the load. Engines are usually provided with a separate battery for starting so that you always have power available for that vital operation.

'...Wind and water chargers can be used at sea to help keep the batteries topped up.'

Seasickness

You don't need to be put off cruising by seasickness. I know how debilitating it can be, having suffered from it for 60 years, but I find that taking the tablets well before departure sorts things out. In my experience, most people who say that the tablets do not work have not taken them early enough. I find that an hour before departure is about right and since I discovered that I have not had a problem and have enjoyed many days of serious and pleasurable cruising.

I am not dedicated to one particular type of seasickness tablet and for me they all seem to work. The only downside is that you can feel more tired than normal after taking the tablets, so it is a good idea to have someone on board who can take over the watch while you have a quick nap. After that everything should be fine.

There is no shame in seasickness and if one of your crew is prone, insist that they take a tablet; this can be something to mention at the crew briefing. Keep an eye on your crew at sea and if you see one of them showing signs of seasickness then be sympathetic. They will want to be in the fresh air but only let them sit in the cockpit if they are secured with a lifeline. In bad cases of seasickness people can lose total responsibility for their actions.
The best thing is to give any sufferer a place on the boat where they have a view forward and can see the horizon. Seasickness is reckoned to be caused by the brain receiving conflicting messages from your eyes and the balance system in your ears. The balance system says you are moving but your eyes say you are not if they are focused inside the boat. With the horizon in view, things appear to be more normal.

The open air of the cockpit can help with seasickness but any sufferers must be secured with a lifeline.

Operating the boat

The standard cockpit layout of a bench seat on either side has stood the test of time and there may be a portable table in the centre so you can eat out here in fine weather. This table is best stowed away at sea because it can restrict free movement about the cockpit and partially block the cabin exit. Somewhere to brace your feet can add to comfort when the boat is rolling or heeled well over and I also like handholds, but they tend to be a rare fitting. On small yachts the cockpit can get crowded because it has to be used to sail and steer the yacht, allow the crew to sit out and participate, and also provide a social centre.

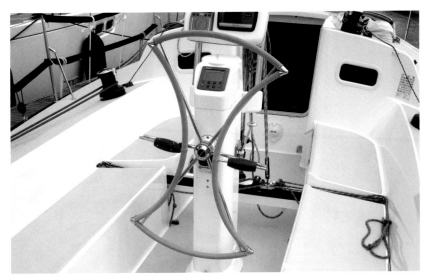

A folding wheel like this creates more space in the cockpit in harbour.

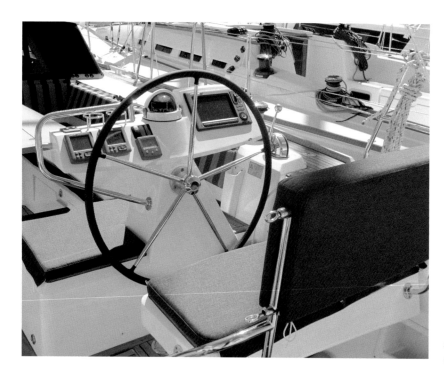

A seat at the helm is a luxury for the helmsman.

The merits of wheel or tiller steering continue to be discussed. With a tiller you have the benefit of simplicity with very little to go wrong as the tiller is connected directly to the rudder stock. You can also have a better 'feel' when sailing the yacht; however, the tiller does take up space in the cockpit as you have to allow room for it to swing from side to side. Today you will only find tillers on smaller yachts, particularly those with a transom hung rudder. With wheel steering there is the complication of translating the movement of the wheel into the required movement of the rudder, which can involve gearing, cables and pulleys or hydraulics. The wheel is usually located well aft so it does not intrude on the cockpit seating. Standing at the wheel and steering a sailboat in a fresh breeze is a great feeling and you certainly get a much better view of the sails and the horizon from this position. Modern yachts use a large wheel that gives you a good sensitive feel of the behaviour of the yacht but that big wheel takes up space in the cockpit and can restrict movement about the yacht in harbour. Some larger yachts have twin wheels so you have a choice on which side to steer, but that is mainly for the cruiser/racer.

When the conditions are lively there can be spray curling into the cockpit over the weather side, particularly when close-hauled. A constant deluge can be debilitating and a small alteration in course may help to reduce the spray. The name canvases fitted to the side rails may offer some protection, although they rarely extend far enough forward. Centre cockpit yachts can reduce the spray problem because you are usually sitting higher up, while some yachts are worse than others with regard to spray because of the hull and deck design. Yacht designers often fit a portable canvas cuddy over the front end of the cockpit or even a fixed open-ended wheelhouse in motorsailer style, and these can make life on board more comfortable and give protection from spray, wind and rain – however, you do feel a little removed from the actions of the boat inside this protection and the visibility can be quite restricted. Also, there may not be the same ready access to the sheets and control ropes as with an open cockpit.

Make sure that the sheets and other ropes have a good lead to the winches.

Sitting in the cockpit

The focus of the action in a sailboat is the cockpit and here there should be space for the whole crew to sit out at the same time. This enables everyone to participate in the sailing and also the fresh air can be a benefit for anyone who is feeling queasy. Most cockpits are designed as safe, secure places for sitting out at sea and here you have most of the ropes and fittings used to control the yacht within easy reach. In fine conditions there is no reason why some crew cannot go out onto the foredeck in the daytime but in adverse conditions and at night the more secure cockpit area is the place to be.

A steering pedestal that incorporates all the navigation instruments.

The cockpit seating should be comfortable when heeled as well as when upright.

Above: A canvas cuddy is a great asset for weather protection that can be folded away in fine weather.

There is rarely room in an open cockpit for a paper chart, which is where modern electronics come into their own. Now they are in watertight cases, electronics can be mounted in the cockpit where the information is readily available, which can be a great benefit when entering harbour or navigating in congested waters. They can work well outside except that they can be prone to reflections on the screen in bright sunlight unless the mounting angle is carefully chosen or an eyebrow is fitted over the top. Rain and spray on the display will also make it difficult to read. The wind and performance instruments and of course that vital compass can also be mounted here, so you have all the information to sail the yacht at your fingertips. The traditional navigation station down below is still important because here you can sit down and consider options and planning away from the hassle of the action in the cockpit, and you might even have a dedicated navigator in your crew who will make this space his home at sea.

Organising the cockpit

You probably cannot do much to change the cockpit layout, because the designer and builder have decided that; you can, however, organise the crew when they are sitting outside. With just two of you sailing, this is easy; but when you have four or five people in the cockpit on a small yacht it requires a bit of discipline as things can get crowded and you still need access to all the fittings such as ropes and winches. This can be a good time to sail the yacht a bit harder so that you tend the sheets on a constant basis and trim the sails to each change of conditions, giving all the crew members something to do.

Left: Having the radio below is fine but it does require a dedicated operator when entering harbour.

Electronic displays

With radar and chart displays you have either a touch screen to control the system or one that uses knobs and push buttons – or possibly a combination of the two. Each has its advantages and disadvantages so if you have a choice about which to use, consider carefully.

With touch screen systems you have to be within reaching distance of the display to make it work. With a conventional layout, with the displays located well in front of you at the helm, this means reaching out to the screen (sometimes through the steering wheel) to make any changes. Touch screen displays are very intuitive to use and when you have experience with iPads and iPhones you feel quite at home.

Most displays that use knobs and buttons for control now have a remote keyboard that you can place anywhere convenient. There are some hybrid systems with both touch screen and knob control but this seems to offer the worst of both worlds rather than the best.

It is difficult to decide which is the better format and this dilemma suggests that we are perhaps at a transit stage of development for marine display screens. A system that is much more intuitive in terms of automatically assessing the navigation situation, such as adjusting the scale automatically to suit the requirements and with radar automatically putting a bearing marker on an approaching vessel, could greatly reduce the requirements for manual control, but this still seems to be some way in the future.

Steering pedestals get ever more complex and this one has the instruments in front of the steering wheel.

Shorts and shirt are great gear for fine weather sailing.

Stabilisers

While many motor cruisers are fitting stabilisers, these power-hungry units have still to reach the sailboat market. Of course, a sailboat has its own built-in stabiliser with the pressure of the wind in the sails doing quite a good job of stabilising the boat. Even on a reach with the wind and sea on the beam the yacht should only roll to a limited extent and the only wind direction where rolling can be a problem is when it is aft. With the wind in this direction the sails do not have the same stabilising effect, and the hull is more prone to rolling in a following sea anyway because the inherent stability of the hull can be considerably reduced when the yacht sits on the crest of a wave. A solution here to make life more comfortable on board could be to alter course several degrees to put the sea more on one quarter or the other.

Dress for the occasion

Wearing the correct clothing makes a huge difference to life on board at sea. Modern foul-weather gear can do a great job of keeping crews both dry and warm, even when faced with constant spray. Much of the modern gear has been designed for the hardy sailors who venture down into the Southern Ocean in long-distance races – and if it works there, it will work anywhere. However, some of these suits are not that easy to get on and off quickly, particularly on a moving boat, so in adverse conditions you will tend to keep it on all the time. It makes sense to get your gear on before you leave harbour – then you will be ready to face whatever conditions you find outside and you can always

Having your foul weather gear on before you leave harbour makes sense in adverse conditions.

take it off in stages if things turn out better than you expected. When it gets cold, as it can in night-time sailing, you need to think about the extremities so warm boots, gloves and head gear are just as important as the main jacket and trousers. Consider the option of wearing several layers, which you can put on or discard as appropriate, rather than having just one thick set of oillies.

A happy crew equals a happy cruise

You want to enjoy your time at sea and life will be much more comfortable if you think about the problems and take steps to make the boat better equipped for passage making. Your first priority should be the safety and comfort of your crew, because if they are happy, life on board will be much more pleasant. There may be limits to what you can do to improve comfort and security, but you can improve the ride in many cases by altering the course or the speed so there is less movement in the boat. Many of the comfort options are in your hands as the skipper, and a cruise need not necessarily be a straight line to the destination at the fastest possible speed. Ease back and enjoy life at sea as well as in harbour.

This is how sailboat cruising should be.

12
Coping with
emergencies

What if...?

In the vast majority of cases you will complete your cruise without any dramas, but there is always a risk of problems even on the most well organised boat, and there is not the ready access to help that you find on land. Fortunately, for every crisis there is a solution.

The best way to prepare for potential problems is to carry out a mental 'what if' exercise before you set out on your cruise, thinking about some of the things that could go wrong and the possible solutions. This exercise is an excellent discipline because if a problem does arise, you will have a much better idea of how to cope.

In most emergency situations, the action you take in the first few minutes determines your long-term capability of dealing with the emergency adequately. In this chapter we will look at some of the scenarios you might encounter while cruising and offer some suggestions about how to cope. These will obviously be general rather than specific, because each boat and situation will demand variations in the course of action. However, these suggestions should give you the incentive to look around your boat and decide how you would translate them appropriately.

Wild winds have blown out both jibs on this cutter yacht.

Hole in the hull

The notion of situations at sea that are likely to produce a hole in the hull conjures up visions of very sudden and dramatic incidents. A collision with a large floating object (such as a tree, a container, or another boat) or going aground are the most likely causes, and how you cope with the hole will depend on both the hull material and the type of hull. With the normal type of GRP hull you are unlikely to get a large hole unless perhaps you hit a floating bulk of timber end on, or the stem of another vessel comes through your topsides. GRP tends not to give way completely and is very resistant to impact, so hull damage incurred through a collision is much more likely to see the section of the hull directly in line with the impact pushed inward, but not give way completely. This means you will get water coming into the hull but hopefully not the sudden catastrophic inflow that could occur with a large hole. Except in a grounding situation it is rare to hit anything with a direct impact, and a glancing blow, while serious, is only likely to generate a series of smaller leaks.

The best solution here is to try to push something like bedding into the leaking area and call for help. There are two schools of thought about when you call for help. Should this be a first reaction to an accident, or should you try to fix the problem on a temporary basis and then call? With two or three crew on board you can split the responsibilities and do both at once, but calling for help is vital once you establish how serious the incident is and there should be no delay. Indeed, calling for help is so important that one of the crew should be detailed at the pre-departure crew briefing to make this his priority.

In addition to trying to curb the inflow you should start the bilge pumps, and if you also have a hand bilge pump system, then use that too. The chances of you sorting out a leaking hull on your own are small and once you have called for help and tried to stem the leak as best you can, it is time to get everybody to put on lifejackets (perhaps they should already have had them on) and to get the liferaft ready. Setting off distress flares can be a useful addition to making contact by radio, but if you have made radio contact, the flares are best kept in reserve to indicate your position to rescuers.

Above: The bilge pump is an essential piece of safety equipment.

Left: Modern Coastguard stations are there to help when you get into trouble at sea.

With modern electronics you can give a position with considerable accuracy, but bear in mind that both the radio and the electronics require electric power and with batteries often mounted low in the boat, these may be the first thing to be covered by the inflow of water. This is where the portable GPS and VHF radio units could be lifesavers.

If grounding has caused the hole, the chances are you will not be going very far and will have to wait for rescue. If the hole has been caused by collision, either with floating debris or another boat, you may still be mobile. Now you have the option of heading for the nearest port (which is a good reason to identify alternative ports in your passage planning, see Chapter 2) or perhaps for the shore, where you may be able to beach the boat. Your particular circumstances will determine the best option and the prevailing weather will also be a factor. You don't necessarily want to beach the boat if there is a fresh onshore wind, but in any emergency situation choices can be very limited.

Another situation, equivalent to a hole in the hull, could be the failure of a seawater inlet pipe, allowing water into the hull. Shutting off the seacocks is the simple solution but bear in mind that as the water floods the hull it is likely to cover the seacocks, so you need to know where these are located and how to gain access to them, even under water – marking their locations is a good precaution.

Above left: The safety margins in a yacht can reduce as the wind increases.

Above right: The crew decided to abandon ship long before it got to this stage.

Grounding

In any grounding situation there are two main priorities. The safety of your crew must be your number one priority so, along with trying to resolve the basic problem, you should also get safety equipment ready for immediate use, and of course make sure a distress call goes out for help from the shore. The other is to try to get an anchor out to at least hold the boat in position and prevent it drifting further ashore. The tender is the only means of doing this unless you have outside help, and you must assess the risks of using the tender in the prevailing conditions before embarking on this undertaking.

Grounding can produce a wide variety of situations, some immediate and serious, others requiring patience and seamanship. The action you take will depend a great deal on the type of bottom on which the yacht goes aground and on the prevailing sea conditions. Going aground in the confines of a harbour or estuary is more likely to hurt your pride than the boat itself and it may be just a question of running the engine astern to try to get the boat off immediately or waiting until the tide floods sufficiently to lift the boat off the bottom. Going aground out in the open sea when there is wave motion is a more serious situation, and going aground on rocks can be even more serious because of the risk of hull damage. The advantage of a sailboat in this situation is that the propeller is rarely the lowest part of the boat so there is every chance you will still have propulsion power available when you go aground.

The first action when a boat grounds is to try to get it off again immediately by going astern. Sailboats do not usually have a great deal of astern thrust but it is always worth a try. If the immediate action to get the boat off is not successful, you need to plan a longer-term strategy. Getting the sails down can prevent the boat blowing further aground but this will depend on the wind direction. Then you need to know what the tide is doing. If it is flooding, maintaining the engine running astern should let the tide lift the boat and hopefully get you out of trouble. In this situation it could be a good idea to lay out an anchor if the boat does not float immediately, in order to prevent the boat drifting further onto the shoal as the tide rises. On a falling tide, you may be able to run out an anchor with the tender in the direction of deeper water; and hauling on this anchor line, together with the use of the engine, may be enough to drag the boat off the shallow bottom before the tide drops too far. Laying out the anchor with the tender can be tricky and the best way to do this is to have the anchor hanging over the side of the dinghy with the chain lashed on board by means of a light line, which can quickly be cut to let the anchor go.

On a falling tide, if your immediate actions have not been enough to get the boat off the bottom you still need to lay out an anchor, particularly if there is any wind blowing. This will prevent the boat blowing harder aground and will also hold the boat head to wind and secure when the tide starts to flow and the boat floats off the bottom. When you do lay out an anchor, try to put out as much scope on the cable as possible to ensure that the anchor holds well, and keep a steady strain on the cable. When the tide eventually starts to lift the boat, steadily wind in the cable as the boat gradually floats off the bottom and you will soon find yourself in deeper water ready to start the engine and hopefully return some sort of normality to the situation. Another option with a deep keel yacht is to swing the boom out to one side and get the crew out there if possible. The weight on the end of the boom might be enough to heel the yacht and reduce the draft sufficiently to get the yacht floating temporarily.

A deep keel yacht will heel over a long way – almost onto its beam ends – if it goes aground, and this could lead to the hull flooding when the tide rises. Make sure there is no leakage from the fuel tank as the boat heels and then, when the tide is flooding, make sure that all the openings – particularly the companionway door – are closed off as far as possible to try to reduce the inflow of water before the hull floats upright.

Towing and being towed

Hopefully, you will be the boat that does the towing rather than the boat being towed, but you may have to face either of these situations at sea and neither operation is an easy one if there are big waves about. Even in calm water towing is quite a skilled operation if it is to work successfully for any distance, and in rough seas it can be an operation fraught with difficulty and danger.

If you have to be towed, you have probably suffered an engine or gear failure or both, although towing could also be necessary in a steering failure situation. With your boat immobile, all the manoeuvring has to be done by the other boat, but you can help by getting things ready and making sure the tow line is secured fast at the first attempt. There is a heavy strain on a tow line, so you need somewhere strong to make it fast. This will probably be the anchor capstan if it is mounted on deck; otherwise, you might take a single turn around a mooring cleat and then take the end around the mast to spread the load. The stresses on the tow line can be very high indeed and even if you use the capstan it is best to take a couple of turns of the towing line around it and then take the end of the line back to a second securing point, such as a mooring cleat. In this way the load is spread throughout the hull instead of being concentrated on one point and this gives a better chance of safely absorbing any heavy snatches on the tow line.

Another option is to use a rope bridle strung between two of the mooring cleats and hanging clear of the bow.

It is a good idea to identify a safe set-up for making fast a tow rope as part of your cruise planning, and you might even like to practise being towed on a fine day, using a friendly boat as the tow boat. Once the tow line is made fast, you may be able to help with the towing operation if you have steering available. This can be used to prevent the boat being towed from sheering about wildly and increasing the strain on the tow line.

Towing a boat is not something to undertake lightly. It calls for skilful manoeuvring and rope handling. The first stage when you have everything ready is to pass a tow rope across and this is best done with your stern level with the bow of the other boat. Manoeuvre close enough for the line to be thrown across, using a lighter line for the initial contact if this is going to be easier to throw. If the sea and wind conditions are difficult and you are reluctant to get this close to the boat you will be towing, as could be the case if it has gone aground, you could float the line down to the other boat using a fender tied to the end of the tow line to keep it afloat and make it visible.

When you are passing the tow line, keep an eye out at all times to make sure the rope does not end up around your propeller – you certainly don't want to compound the situation in this way. The person handling the line on the stern of your boat must allow just enough slack line to enable the line to be passed across and never allow a bight of rope to lie in the water. Try not to use astern gear in this situation. When you are making the line fast on your stern, use a bridle if necessary in order to spread the load between the two stern cleats. It is rare to find a good strong towing point on leisure boats these days and an alternative solution could be to take a couple of turns around a stern cleat and then back it up with further turns around a winch. You want the pull to be focused at the stern.

Take up the weight gently on the tow rope once it is fast and try to keep an even strain, not an easy task in rough seas. Radio contact between the two boats will bring an added measure of safety to the operation. You should be able to find a speed of towing at which both boats are comfortable without too much snatching on the line. In calmer conditions you can keep a reasonably short tow line, but in rougher conditions you need a longer tow line between the two craft to give a bit of spring. You can experiment to find a length that gives a compatible motion between the two craft. If the boat being towed still has steering, a position somewhere just on the quarter of the towing boat can often be a comfortable place to hold. Heavy sheering about of the boat being towed should be avoided because of the great strain it puts on the tow line and the fittings, and the potential that will exist in this situation for the tow line to suffer chafe. Chafe is the enemy of towing operations and rags or other anti-chafe gear should be used where the tow rope rubs.

Mast down

Dismasting is quite rare on a cruising yacht, where the rig should be well stressed for normal operations. The main cause of a dismasting might be poor tensioning of the rigging or possibly an uncontrolled gybe. The first priority in a dismasting is to check that the crew are all OK and then you can set about removing or securing the damaged bits. Having bolt cutters on board will enable you to cut through any of the wires holding the broken section alongside if it went overboard and then let the whole lot go. If you can

A mast coming down can be a traumatic experience for the crew.

disconnect the sails from the broken section, all well and good; but there is not a lot of point in trying to salvage much from the wreckage. It is more important to try to dispose of the mast sections and rigging if they are alongside the hull in the water before they do any damage to the hull and compound the situation. If the mast has fallen down onto the deck, it is best to try to tidy things up and secure the bits; but a broken mast is unlikely to be repairable, so salvaging will not be a high priority.

If you are coastal cruising, or just on a slightly longer than usual passage, the engine should be enough to get you to a safe harbour. On a longer deep-sea passage you may need to think about rigging some sort of jury rig if there is not enough fuel to get you to harbour. There may be some of the mast left upright to act as the support for a jury rig or you could use the boom or the spinnaker pole. It requires a lot of ingenuity to get something that works and you might want to call for help instead. As always in any emergency, an early call on the radio at least to inform the Coastguard of your predicament is a good idea.

Engine failure

An engine failure on a sailboat out at sea should not be the end of the world and you should at least be able to sail close to your destination. From there you can get on the radio to the marina or harbour authorities and arrange a tow in. If you are skilled, have a competent crew and are going to pick up a mooring, entering harbour under sail alone is an option; however, you cannot sail into a marina berth so in this case you will need to pick up a tow at some stage of the final journey.

You should have the tools on board to cope with some of the basic causes of engine failure. Modern diesel engines need both an electrical supply and clean fuel to keep going. Failure of the electrical supply to the engine could be a blown fuse or an open breaker and you should know where these are located so you can fix them quickly. Regarding the fuel, about the most you can do is check that the fuel filters are clean and there is no water in the fuel, which you can normally see in the glass filter bowl. Modern computer-controlled engines will often show what the problem is on the electronic display and this may give you a clue as to what to do to cure the problem, but with modern engines you tend to be very limited in what can be achieved in the way of repairs beyond bleeding the fuel system.

One problem that can cause serious disruption away from the engine itself is a failure in the seawater cooling system. This system brings seawater in through a seacock and then a strainer, and on into the heat exchanger where the seawater cools the fresh water in the engine cooling. After the engine cooling the seawater may go on to cool the gearbox oil and it is then injected into the exhaust system where it cools the hot exhaust gases and prevents them from burning through the rubber exhaust pipes. So this seawater has a vital role to play in keeping everything running.

If the seawater supply fails, perhaps through a burst inlet pipe or a blocked inlet, the problems start to escalate rapidly. Firstly, you could have water starting to flood the engine compartment. Then the engine will start to overheat, possibly followed by a fire starting in the rubber exhaust pipe as that overheats. This is a worst-case scenario, all because one hosepipe has failed! The first warning you have will be the engine temperature rising, but by the time you notice this, the damage may have been done and the exhaust pipe is on fire. The cure is to stop the engine and shut the intake seacock, but will you be able to get access to the seacock when it may be underwater and when the engine compartment is full of burning rubber fumes? Do you put out the fire first and then try to stop the water inflow? You do need to think this one through carefully. Extending the seacock spindles to a point outside the engine compartment is one solution, and in terms of prevention it is a good idea to change the engine hoses at regular intervals. I have not experienced such a situation on a boat but it is one of the wide variety of scenarios of what could go wrong.

'...it is a good idea to change the engine hoses at regular intervals.'

Loss of steering

Loss of the steering is a frustrating and potentially dangerous situation. The failure may be in the operating mechanism that connects the wheel to the rudder, in which case there is often a square head on the rudder stock where you can fit a temporary tiller. If it is the rudder that has failed in some way, you have a more serious problem on your hands; but if your engine is an outboard, as it can be on a small yacht, then you have an emergency form of steering there. A bow thruster, if you have one, could also give you emergency steering but you will need to have the engine running as there will be a heavy drain on the battery. Otherwise you have the option of trying to set the sails so you can exercise some steering control by adjusting the balance of the sails or you can try to rig some form of jury steering – or, of course, you can call for assistance.

A bow thruster can provide a good form of emergency steering if the rudder fails.

Rigging jury steering will not be easy because you are unlikely to have anything on board suitable for the job. You could rig the spinnaker pole hinged over the stern with some form of blade attached or you might be able to rig ropes with perhaps a bucket attached where you can switch the pull from the rope from side to side. Here is a situation where that call for help could bring you tow assistance to get you into harbour.

Fire

Fire at sea is a frightening experience, and on board a yacht there are plenty of highly combustible materials to fuel a fire. Prevention is obviously better than cure, a phrase easier to say than to adopt. There are four main areas where fire is likely to start: in the accommodation, the galley, the engine compartment, and the electrical circuits. Fire in the accommodation is most likely to be caused by smoking, so strict control of smoking on board and a discipline to ensure that lighted cigarette ends are not left around the boat will help to prevent this situation. In the galley there are always risks where flame or hot cooking rings exist and the galley should never be left unattended when something is cooking on the stove. Hot oil in the frying pan is usually the culprit here and it is wise to avoid cooking this way at sea.

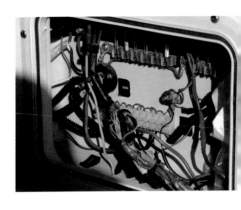

The electrical system can be the cause of a fire if connections spark or wires get chafed.

Electrical circuits probably provide the greatest fire hazard on board modern boats, mainly because the wiring is mostly hidden out of sight so any problem is not visible. The risk here comes from short circuits caused perhaps by wires chafing, which can create enough heat and sparks to start a fire. All electrical circuits should be protected by fuses or breakers, which will greatly reduce the chance of fire if a circuit does prove faulty because they isolate that particular circuit automatically. One of the main fire risk areas is in the heavy-duty battery cables, which are not protected by fuses or breakers, and these need to be very carefully installed and maintained, as do the batteries themselves, if the risk of fire is to be minimised. So often I have come across batteries that are not fully secured and any movement here can cause the heavy-duty cables to spark and possibly start a fire. Another point with batteries is that they are often stowed low in the boat to lower the centre of gravity. This means that if the engine room is flooded, batteries are likely to be one of the first things to go underwater and then you can lose both your bilge pumps and your radio communications just when you might need them.

In the engine compartment, apart from the electrical risks there is the scenario of the seawater intake failure detailed above, which could start a fire, and the fuel can also present a danger if it leaks, particularly a leak in the high pressure part of modern common rail systems. Boats are normally fitted with some means of isolating the fuel tanks from outside the engine compartment, and with the fuel cut off in this way the fire will not be fed by further fuel and

The intensity of a fire inside the hull can be judged by this exterior blistering of the paintwork.

you have some chance of coping. Most modern boats also have an extinguishing system for the engine compartment, operated by remote control. Switch off the engines and try to block off any air inlets before using this, as the engine will draw in air, which will feed the fire. If you do operate such a system, leave it for some time before opening to assess the situation. The fire can so easily start up again with a fresh input of oxygen and your extinguishing system does not have a second shot.

Provided it is discovered early and you have appropriate extinguishers, the fire itself should not be too much of a hazard.

The risks from fire tend to come from the associated smoke and fumes rather than from the flames themselves. Bunk cushions and other furnishings can generate large quantities of toxic fumes when on fire, and an electrical short circuit behind panelling could have the same effect if there is foam insulation. These fumes can be so dense that they can force the crew to evacuate the compartment and then you can't get to the seat of the fire to tackle it and the situation can escalate rapidly. I have experienced this off Lizard Point at night when we were ripping down panelling to find the seat of the fire and all the time being driven back by the dense fumes.

Extinguishing the fire

Fire extinguishers should always be located outside the compartment they are meant to protect. This allows you to tackle the fire from outside, which in turn keeps your escape route open. If you suspect that the fire is electrical in origin, turn off the batteries at the main switch to try to isolate the circuits so that the initial cause of the fire is removed. In a galley fire, try to switch off the gas or other combustibles, so once again the basic fuel for the fire is removed. In the engine compartment, both fuel and electrical circuits should be isolated. If you get to the fire early enough, an extinguisher should be adequate to put out the fire, but remember that on a boat you are not dealing with a nice, comfortable, stable situation.

One of your first reactions on discovering a fire will probably be to stop the engine, if it is running, or head up into the wind. You need to find a delicate balance between having fire extinguishers that have adequate capacity to cope with a severe fire but are light enough to operate one-handed, because you may need the other hand for holding on. The best type of boat fire extinguisher is the one where the discharge can be controlled so that you fire off just enough of the extinguishing gas or liquid to control the fire, but have a reserve left in case it flares up again. Obviously you need more than one fire extinguisher, and others can be brought to the fire ready for use, but the supply of extinguishers on a boat is always limited and you must try to use them as effectively as possible and keep something in reserve.

You are, of course, surrounded by one of the best fire-fighting mediums, which is water. This will cope with most fires on board except those involving fuel, electricity and probably galley fires. While the fire is being tackled by fire extinguishers, have buckets of water ready in the cockpit to reinforce the fire extinguishers. It may make a mess but that is far preferable to having the boat burned down to the waterline. If the fire is in a mattress or other bedding, the most expedient way of dealing with it may be simply to drag the offending item out into the cockpit and dump it overboard.

The fumes generated by a fire are likely to be much more of a problem than the actual fire itself and if they become a major problem, then one approach is to seal off the compartment involved, blanking off as many ventilators and openings as possible, and simply let the fire burn itself out because it will now be starved of oxygen. Make sure that you have all the crew out from down below and try to keep one part of the boat still habitable in a fire situation. It may be possible to control the spread of the fumes to a certain extent by running downwind, which will tend to keep the stern of the boat clear. In any fire situation, the priorities should be first to tackle the fire as quickly as possible and secondly to send off a distress message, perhaps using that portable VHF if the main batteries have been switched off.

Top Tip

Adding fuel to the fire

For a fire to burn it needs oxygen, heat and fuel. Take away one of these and the fire will go out. For instance, water put on a fire will remove heat by generating steam, and this steam in turn will displace the oxygen, making water a good fire-extinguishing medium (except for electrical fires). Fire extinguishers tend to work in different ways but most work on the basis of excluding the oxygen, which will stop the fire burning. However, there is always the risk here that once the extinguishing gas or liquid has dispersed, oxygen will be able to get back to the seat of the fire and you can find the fire flaring up again after it has apparently been extinguished. This is because the other two factors required for fire – heat and fuel – have not been eliminated.

Abandoning ship

There are three main situations where you may be forced to consider abandoning ship. One is when the vessel is on fire; another is when you have suffered a failure of machinery or steering and the boat is drifting ashore; and the final one is when the boat is holed or sinking. These can all be pretty desperate situations, but even so you want to save making the transition from the boat into the liferaft until the last possible minute. Taking to the liferaft is an irrevocable step that doesn't offer you immediate salvation, and you will always be better off staying on board the boat while it remains tenable and afloat.

Taking to the liferaft when the yacht is on fire poses particular problems. In any evacuation situation it would be normal to put the liferaft over on the lee side, which not only helps to make boarding easier but also allows the liferaft to drift away downwind once the crew is on board. With the boat on fire the lee side is the last place you want to be, because smoke and flames will blow down to leeward. If you put the liferaft over on the windward side, it is less at risk from the fire, but getting away from the side will be very difficult. The alternative and probably the best solution in this situation is to put the liferaft over at either the bow or the stern, depending on the heading of the yacht and where the seat of the fire is located.

The key to successful evacuation in a fire situation is to make an early decision to evacuate. Almost certainly a fire will have started down below in the accommodation or the engine compartment rather than on deck, and if you resolve to abandon ship before the fire spreads to the hull and superstructure you should have a good chance of getting out safely. If you wait until the last possible moment, when flames are raging in the cockpit or through cabin windows, your chances of a safe evacuation are considerably reduced. The time to evacuate is when you have lost control in fighting the fire. In other words, if you have exhausted all the fire extinguishers and other means of extinguishing the blaze and the fire is still growing, there is little more you can do except look after your own safety – and in that situation, the sooner you get into the liferaft, the better.

Left: The liferaft should be stowed in an easily accessible position.

Below: The inflated liferaft can provide a means of escape but should only be used as a last resort.

Just trying to launch a liferaft can be a struggle. The instructions tell you to pick up the liferaft and throw it overboard. Try doing this in harbour and you might be struggling. Doing it at sea with the boat rolling heavily can be a real challenge, so this is something to try out long before you need it for real, and do make sure that the liferaft painter is always attached so that the raft will not drift off before you get into it. It is the pull on this painter that inflates the liferaft so it is the vital connection between you and the raft. Put as much as you can in the way of stores and useful equipment into the raft, not forgetting that vital handheld VHF and possibly a portable GPS so that you can talk to would-be rescuers and give a position. A grab bag ready with all the necessities can be a good thing to keep handy in the cockpit.

Man overboard

At first glance, having one of your crew fall overboard seems a straightforward matter to deal with. You simply turn round, head back, pick him up and away you go. But behind this apparently straightforward plan lies a whole host of difficulties – you have to locate the person in the water, control your boat and bring it back to the man overboard (something not always easy to achieve), and then, probably the most difficult of all, you have to get the person back on board. The situation can turn into a nightmare where lives are at risk, and things can quickly get out of hand.

The first action to take when someone goes overboard is to release or throw a marker. If you have a lifebuoy or dan marker buoy at the stern then let this go or, failing that, a cockpit cushion could help. The thing you throw may offer buoyancy, and will also make it easier to keep the person in the water in sight – by the time you have turned to come back again, finding that person among the waves can be a difficult and frustrating task. At night-time the problem is compounded because without some form of light to indicate the position, finding someone in the water is even more difficult.

A selection of man overboard gear on the stern of this sailboat.

The next step is to post one of the crew on deck whose sole task is to keep sight of the person in the water. This requires concentration and he should not be distracted from this task for any reason because once you lose sight, finding the person again will be that much more difficult. If you have an electronic chart, press the Man Overboard button and this will record the GPS position just in case.

Turning round quickly under sail can be a challenge and it is best to switch on the engine and to a certain extent let the sails take care of themselves. There are set procedures for turning round to pick up someone who has gone overboard, but on a cruising yacht just switching on the engine and going astern could be the best solution as you will remain near the casualty. There is nothing more reassuring than seeing the boat stop and return quickly, which lets him know that not only has he been spotted but that recovery is imminent. Seeing a boat going away in a wide sweeping turn can be quite alarming and could lead to the person in the water panicking, reducing his chances of survival.

Having got back to the man overboard, you are still faced with the problem of recovery. The best recovery position can be at the stern but this is very close to the propeller and there is also the risk of the casualty going under the stern. You can stop upwind and drift down and if the conditions are suitable you could launch the tender. If the casualty is conscious and fit, throwing a line to him could help a lot; but you still have the problem of lifting the person on board. To lift them physically can be extremely difficult and a rope bight at the end of the topping lift or a halyard can help enormously. All these things are easy to say but hard to execute; and the situation can be a lot worse if there were just two of you on board. In a worst-case scenario you may at least be able to secure the casualty alongside and wait for help to arrive. As always, calling for help at an early stage is a wise move.

Where the crew might be most at risk of going overboard is when they are dealing with some other emergency on board and fail to observe the normal safety precautions. Insisting on lifelines being worn even in the cockpit can reduce the risk – you might still go overboard with a lifeline if it is long enough but at least you are connected to the boat, which will help recovery. It is important to slow the boat down quickly if this does happen. In any sort of adverse conditions, insist that the crew also wear lifejackets. At least then they will have a better chance of survival if they are in the water and they will be easier to see, particularly at night if the lifejacket has a light.

Prevention is better than cure

There is no such thing as absolute safety at sea when you are cruising. Experience is a great asset in dealing with emergencies which can develop quickly and suddenly and require an instant response. Practice in safety and survival procedures as far as is practical is vital to success in an emergency and helps to develop an awareness of what is required and of the risks involved in boating of all types. Safety is not just a question of having the right equipment on board – it is knowing how and when to use it, as well as thinking through how you would cope with various emergencies. The consequences of things going wrong can strengthen both your resolve and your on-board discipline to avoid situations where emergency procedures are required. Prevention is obviously much better than cure and while the routines necessary to avoid disaster may at times appear tedious and over-cautious, you must remember that the sea is a hard taskmaster. If you let down your guard, the sea and the conditions you find there are just waiting to take advantage of your weaknesses.

The swim ladder that is shown stowed away here can provide a great means of recovering a man overboard.

Good equipment and personal gear are essential for safety at sea.

13
Rules and regulations

The COLREGs

One of the attractions of cruising is that you escape from the increasing restrictions on the freedom of life ashore. Out at sea you are largely on your own and you decide the levels of safety and security you enforce on board. However, you cannot escape entirely from rules and regulations at sea.

The main set of rules that affect you are the COLREGs, which not only control your actions when you have an encounter with another vessel but also dictate what lights and shapes you should carry to indicate the type of vessel you are, and also your behaviour in poor visibility. It is a set of rules developed from experience and in recent years they have expanded considerably to encompass the use of electronic systems and to cover new types of vessels such as WIGS and hovercraft. These rules are designed to cover most situations you are likely to experience at sea and when you read them they can appear complex and not easy to understand, but that is because they have a legal standing and lawyers are known to choose their words carefully.

If you are going to operate a boat at sea, as you will when cruising, you must have a good understanding of the rules. When I first went to sea we had to learn the COLREGs off by heart, but thankfully 60 years ago they were not as complex as they are today. Fortunately, there are good books dedicated to explaining the rules and what they mean for yachtsmen and you need to study these in some detail so you are not taken by surprise when you pick up a vessel with strange-looking lights a couple of miles away, and left wondering

Good navigation lights are essential and the rules allow them to be brighter than demanded.

Rule 2

The COLREGs accept that the rules cannot cover every situation that can occur at sea and they have a get-out clause for situations not directly defined in the rules. Rule 2 is perhaps the most important of all and, if you read nothing else, at least take this one on board:

'Nothing in these Rules shall exonerate any vessel or the owner, master or crew thereof, from the consequences of any neglect to comply with these Rules or of the neglect of any precaution that may be required by the ordinary practice of seamen, or by the special circumstances of the case.

In construing and applying these Rules due regard shall be had to all dangers of navigation and collision and to all special circumstances, including the limitations of the vessels involved, which may make a departure from these Rules necessary to avoid immediate danger.'

So there you are – you must follow the Rules but still apply common sense to any situation you find yourself in, and it is Rule 2 that allows you to take early and sensible action to avoid danger and above all to behave in a seamanlike manner. 'Seamanship' sounds such an old-fashioned word these days, but if you are cruising in a serious way then all your actions, those required by the Rules and those that ensure a safe passage, should be governed by sensible seamanship.

☑ Top Tip

Radar and Rule 7(b)

The COLREGs demand that you use your radar effectively if you have one fitted and working. This is covered in Rule 7(b), which states: 'Proper use shall be made of radar equipment if fitted and operational, including long range scanning to obtain early warning of the risk of collision and radar plotting or equivalent systematic observation of detected objects.' So it is not just a case of having your radar on – you must also use it effectively and there are no excuses for not using it.

Fishing boats can show confusing lights at night and are best given a wide berth.

what to do. While the rules are quite clear and precise as to what you should or should not do and the lights that vessels should carry, confusion can still reign. This will mainly come from vessels like fishing boats that may have the proper lights in place but also have bright working lights that make it impossible to distinguish the navigation lights. In daylight, fishing boats should have shapes to indicate the type of fishing they are engaged in, but you find fishing boats in harbour still showing these shapes so there is abuse of the rules in this way. It is also very hard to pick out the navigation lights on passenger ships when they are lit up like Christmas trees. Expect the unexpected when you are out at sea in daylight, and even more so at night; err on the side of safety and give a wide berth to anything you are not sure about.

You need both a licence for the operator and one for the yacht when a radio is fitted.

Enforcement of the COLREGs

There is virtually no process for enforcing the COLREGs. I would like to think that your boatbuilder has fitted navigation lights of suitable power and in the right places according to the rules, but don't take this for granted. I have seen a couple of new boats where the positions of the masthead white light (for use when under power) and the stern light have been reversed, and side lights are not always fitted in suitable places and at suitable angles for maximum effectiveness. I would suggest you read the light rules carefully and check that your lights comply; and there is nothing to stop you fitting lights that are brighter than those demanded by the rules so you will be more visible to other vessels – but remember that they may take more power from your batteries.

There is one area where you may find quite strict enforcement of the Rules, and that is in the Dover Straits. Here the Coastguard keeps a watchful eye on the shipping passing through these narrows, and they will come down heavily on yachts that do not stick to the rules. This includes making sure that if you are crossing the main shipping lanes, you do so with a HEADING at right angles to the shipping lanes. Note the emphasis on 'heading', because that is what the rules demand – it is the heading of your yacht that has to be at right angles, not the course made good. Sailing yachts of any size can use the inshore channels, so this is where you should be unless crossing over – and if you do cross, then it is up to you to keep out of the way of vessels using the traffic lanes, even though you are a sailing boat. Again, you need to know the rules in some detail to make sure you do not offend.

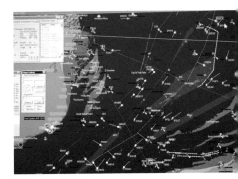

A composite radar picture of the dense shipping in the Dover Straits where special rules apply.

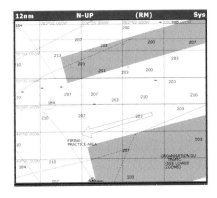

The separation zones on the chart are best avoided by sailing yachts where possible.

Accident investigation

The only other measure of enforcement is likely to come after you have had an accident. This is when your actions will be investigated in depth, and if you are found wanting you are for the high jump. In Britain, the Marine Accident Investigation Branch carries out investigations into accidents and you are under an obligation to report any accident where there has been personal injury. Other countries have similar organisations for accident investigation, so there is no hiding place. If there is only damage to your boat, quite likely it will be your insurance company that wants to know all the details.

Insurance

Insurance is vital when you are cruising, not only to give you peace of mind if things go wrong, but because many marinas will demand to see that you have at least third party insurance of around £3 million before you can be accepted there. If you plan to go foreign, make sure you have coverage for this; some insurance companies require you to inform them of your intentions before you go. Also check your insurance policy carefully before you leave on any cruise because some have limitations on when and how you can cruise. Be sure that your insurance policy gives you cover for personal injury to your crew and to any third party who may suffer from your actions, such as in a collision.

Cruising at home and abroad

Cruising in your own country is generally quite straightforward and in Britain there are no requirements for the boat to be either registered or licensed; nor are the crew required to have any qualifications. The only licence required is for the radio – both for the installation itself and for the user. The radio operator's licence usually demands a one-day course and ideally at least two of the crew should hold this qualification. There is no formal requirement to have at least one or indeed any experienced or qualified person on board, but to my mind it makes sense to have at least two so that if one is incapacitated for any reason, or simply wants to have a sleep, there is someone experienced to take over the watch.

You have to wonder how much longer this non-demand for qualifications will last in Britain because most other countries now require both boat and crew to have some form of licence. This can put British boat owners in a dilemma when they want to cruise abroad and it is necessary to register the boat under the Small Ships Registry (this applies to boats less than 24 metres in length). For a relatively small fee you will have a document certifying that your boat is British, which will satisfy the requirements of most foreign countries.

Most European countries also require that the skipper has some form of licence and the basic qualification here is the International Certificate of Competence. You will qualify for this if you have a Day Skipper's Licence or anything more advanced such as a Yachtmaster, and many owners and their insurance companies feel more comfortable if they have some form of qualification anyway. To qualify for these certificates you need a basic understanding of the COLREGs and buoyage systems, as well as the basics of navigation and boat handling. The basic qualifications are not too demanding and as a boat owner you should have the necessary skills anyway. There are courses available, lasting for a few days or a week, to obtain these qualifications and you can do much of the theory in evening classes in the winter; but some practical experience in boat handling is also

> *'...check your insurance policy carefully before you leave.'*

Above: You need to respect any local regulations in ports that you visit.

Above left: In most countries police, customs and coastguard all have the power to stop you at sea.

Above right: Heading to the police station to clear outwards before leaving a country.

Below: When cruising, rules and regulations can seem a million miles away but you still need to respect them.

demanded. The International Certificate of Competence works fine if you are staying in ports and the open seas, but if you plan to take to the inland waterways you will need to pass a short written test in the special rules that apply there to get a suitable endorsement.

To travel to and from EU countries, you will need to be able to show that you have paid VAT on the boat. This means you will need some form of documentation, such as the purchase invoice and receipt, on board at all times. These days you are largely free to travel anywhere within the EU borders without any further documentation as long as you and the crew take your passports and an EU health insurance card; but in countries outside the EU you will have to go through customs and immigration formalities. Provided your paperwork is in order – and the papers should include a crew list showing full names, nationalities, date of birth and passport numbers – this should not pose any problems, although it can be time consuming.

If you have arrived in Britain from a non-EU country, including the Channel Islands, you will need to go through customs and possibly immigration formalities on arrival. It is the same in all countries if you have a non-EU national on board. Tread carefully if you plan to charter your yacht because in this instance all the rules are tightened up considerably and in some European countries you could be liable for taxes and here you need to take local advice about the situation because it can vary from country to country even in the EU. You will also need to check carefully if you plan to leave your yacht in a foreign port for any length of time because again there could be a tax liability.

So the rules affecting the operation of a boat on a cruise are not too onerous and most are very straightforward and the sort of things you should be on top of anyway. It does make sense to have some form of documentation, some form of qualification, and certainly insurance for your cruising, and the requirements are generally far less strict than you find onshore. There is still a great freedom when you leave harbour but with that freedom comes responsibility and you must approach any cruise with serious intent – but that should not detract from the pleasure. There can be so much pleasure, and for me one of the most satisfying things in life is to complete a cruise in good order so you will enjoy that first beer when you step on shore or sit in the cockpit watching the sunset.

Index